CHURCH IT

USING INFORMATION TECHNOLOGY
FOR THE MISSION OF THE CHURCH

NICK B. NICHOLAOU

A Church Law & Tax Resource from Christianity Today

Published by Christianity Today International
ChristianityToday.org
ChurchLawAndTax.com

All website references were current at the date of publication.

Editors: Jim Bolton, Michelle Dowell
Art Director: Vasil Nazar
Illustrations and Cover Design: Rick Szuecs
Cover image: Akira Hojo on Unsplash

ISBN: 978-0-917463-82-2

Printed in the United States of America

So many churches and ministries have invited me to help them over the last thirty years! I am thankful to each, and dedicate this book to The Bride of Christ, and to God's best gifts to me: my amazing wife and delightful daughter.

Contents

Foreword

In the 1980s, I was privileged to lead what is now called Christian Camp and Conference Association. Back then, every camping leader was scrambling to ensure the computer age didn't leave them in the dust.

Most of us had a-friend-of-a-friend-of-Cousin-Eddie who gave us bad advice. I knew nothing, but I bought my first computer anyway—a Kaypro II. Few things in life are transformational. That machine was!

Fast forward to 1990 when I joined the management team at Willow Creek Community Church. The church had two IT guys then. The soft-spoken one installed a new computer in my office. With the bedside manner of a caring surgeon, he assured me my lack of technology savvy would not matter.

Gratefully, the church loaned us its IT team when we launched Willow Creek Association in 1992. We had an early version of an internal email system, but dozens of those pink "While You Were Out" phone message slips still ended up on my desk. We didn't leverage technology well.

During a Chicago snowstorm in early 1994, a headhunter from sunny California called me about leading Christian Management Association (now called Christian Leadership Alliance). I called my wife from the office and when I arrived home that evening, she was packed!

I'm sharing all of this to say, with deep appreciation, that when I arrived in Southern California, Nick Nicholaou was there to assure me that IT would be the *least* of my worries at CMA. *He was right!*

Nick's amazing firm, Ministry Business Services Inc., ensured that CMA—while seeking to model God-honoring management practices to thousands of church and ministry leaders—would *also* walk the talk and employ God-honoring IT practices in our national office and in our national conferences.

As CMA's national section leader for IT, Nick's mind and heart created a ripple effect of Kingdom fruitfulness.

Malcolm Gladwell's bestseller, *Outliers: The Story of Success,* notes the extraordinary power of the 10,000-hour rule. Gladwell would label Nick a "10,000-hour expert" based on the immense time Nick has invested with churches and ministries across the country. *He has seen it all—the good, the bad, and the ugly, yet he still has a contagious positivity about ministry.* Amazing!

So, without hesitation, I commend this very, very practical book to you. It is high time that a national leader elevated the foundational and critical work of IT! Nick gives you the information—and the why. His warm appreciation for the ministry of IT oozes out because of his high regard for the thousands of miracle-working IT people in the trenches.

So read and share this book with others: your pastor or boss, your colleagues, your volunteers, and your team members (if you have any!). Point out the helpful glossary in the back (a life-saver for me!) and the numerous resources.

When Rolla P. Huff was named president and CEO of EarthLink in 2007, *The Wall Street Journal* highlighted his priorities, which underlined the importance of an organization's operational side (including IT). Huff said,

"It's all about execution.
At the end of the day, I won't be judged
on my plan as much as my execution."

Nick's insightful book will help you execute with excellence. And along the way, be sure to encourage and mentor others—like you—who are called by God to deploy the spiritual gift of administration.

John Pearson
Board Governance & Management Consultant
Author, *Mastering the Management Bucket*

Introduction

In my role as president of MBS, Inc., I've enjoyed the great privilege of serving Christian churches and ministries as an IT consultant and strategist. I started in that role in 1987 and helped churches through a number of IT transitions, including answering these questions:

1. *Should a church buy a computer?* In 1987 most churches wrestled with why a church would want a computer. At that time computers were very expensive, and owning one seemed eccentric! Very few churches had computers. A few subscribed to service bureaus, which is similar to today's hosted computing. Answering this question was my first area of focus in IT consulting, writing, and speaking.

2. *Who on the church staff should have a computer?* As churches began buying and using computers and saw how helpful they were, my next focus was to help them decide which church staff should get computers. Back then a basic desktop computer cost about $5,000! It was an issue of stewardship. For larger churches, giving computers to the finance department was a no-brainer; creating spreadsheets and the ability to automate check writing and contribution statements was easily justified. But what about other staff? Was giving them computers wasteful?

3. *Why should computers be networked?* Once churches began to recognize the value of using computers, many added computers for key staff. My next focus became the why's and how's of connecting computers together. The big question churches asked was, *Why would you want to connect your computers?* In

the early days of networking there were so many new options and methods of connecting computers that it was a confusing choice. The strategic component of my work began to develop bigger muscles as I researched and determined what worked best and for the most reasonable cost. My focus was a mix of being practical and strategic, while balancing church budget sensitivities.

4. *Should a church be on the internet?* When public access to the internet became available through the World Wide Web (www), churches wrestled with website and email issues—and this expanded my focus again. In the mid-1990s, Steve Hewitt, then Editor-in-Chief for *Christian Computing Magazine* (now *MinistryTech Magazine*), and I predicted there would come a day when you would see website addresses in television ads and on the sides of trucks! People were shocked and openly mocked us!

5. *What is virtualization, and should churches use that technology?* When virtualization came along, my focus expanded again to include virtualized computers and servers. This technology saves so much money while increasing reliability and productivity, and improving disaster recovery!

6. *Should churches use cloud technology?* Around 2009, I sensed that the Lord wanted me to strategically help churches move into the cloud. Just as he used me to help develop the *best practices* in each earlier phase of church computing, my impression was that he wanted me and my team to focus on helping bring churches into the cloud.

At each of these stages, the Lord gave me wisdom to identify good hardware, software, and platform strategies that were not biased toward any one vendor. He has given me the privilege of serving many hundreds of churches directly and countless thousands indirectly through my writing and speaking at regional and national conferences.

The Purpose of This Book

This book is specific to IT in church and ministry environments. The church and ministry computing environment is unique. Through my work with churches, I have seen what churches do about IT issues that is *not* strategic. In the pages ahead, I address a number of the most common and costly IT mistakes churches make, with the hope that this book will help many church leaders think through better, more strategic approaches for applying computer technology to the mission of their churches—unique as their computing environments may be.

SECTION ONE

Church IT's Mission

||||||||||||||

When you have vision, it affects your attitude. Your attitude is optimistic rather than pessimistic. ... This is nothing more than having a strong belief in the power of God; having confidence in others around you who are in similar battles with you; and, yes, having confidence in yourself, by the grace of God.

Charles R. Swindoll [1]

||||||||||||||

[1] Swindoll, C. R. (2007), *Dear Graduate: Letters of Wisdom from Charles R. Swindoll,* Nashville, TN, U.S.: Thomas Nelson, Inc.

CHAPTER 1

IT Department Structure

||||||||||||||

The work is too heavy for you; you cannot
handle it alone. (NIV)

Jethro, Moses' father-in-law [2]

||||||||||||||

There are four different technology "knowledge and skill" disciplines in most churches. Often church leadership thinks of them all as IT (Information Technology). That is probably because they all rely heavily on computer technology, and the assumption is that anyone involved in any of the four disciplines is equally capable of serving *in* any of the four areas.

However, each discipline uses different skills and tools. Unfortunately, churches often mistakenly group all four disciplines together into one "IT Department" and select a person strong in one of those disciplines to lead all four. It is one of the most common IT mistakes churches make.

The Four Disciplines of Church Technology

The four disciplines are (1) web and graphic design; (2) audio/video (A/V); (3) social media; and (4) data infrastructure (the design and connecting of systems to ensure appropriate data flow at all levels).

---

[2] Exodus 18:18.

There are exceptions to each of these generalities. But the generalities also reveal some of the dominant characteristics of the people who specialize in each IT discipline.

1. *Web and Graphic Design*. Wikipedia describes this discipline as "the process of visual communication and problem-solving through the use of typography, photography, and illustration."[3] It is similar to designing magazine ads that powerfully communicate a coordinated message all in one graphic, with the goal of moving the viewer toward an action. People who excel in this area are usually articulate communicators who are also very artistic. They use applications to draw, design, and do layout. They are often good project managers because of the timelines and project complexities involved in their work, but they are usually not highly skilled in A/V or data infrastructure, for instance.

2. *Audio/Video*. A/V people are also creative communicators. They specialize in cameras, projection systems, soundboards, systems control boards, and storyboarding. Also good project managers, they can plan the A/V elements of a production from start to finish and make certain all is ready at showtime. The computers used to render videos require a lot of resources and are often more powerful than some servers! Because A/V people use high-quality computers and are usually articulate communicators, they are often tasked with IT oversight. But, like web and graphics people, they are usually not highly skilled in some of the other technology disciplines.

---

3   Wikipedia, https://en.wikipedia.org/wiki/Graphic_design.

3. *Social Media.* Social media people are gifted communicators. They are highly skilled at leveraging today's electronic communication mediums (Twitter, Instagram, Facebook, and so on) to begin and engage in conversations with a wide audience. Their tool is the written word, and although layout sometimes comes into play, they are usually not highly skilled in web and graphic design, A/V, or in the data infrastructure required to connect them with the world. Jonathan Smith, Director of Technology at Faith Ministries in Lafayette, Indiana, said social media is often combined with web and graphic design or data infrastructure because people in those disciplines use social medial tools. But that often is a poor fit. It is best treated separately, he said.

4. *Data Infrastructure.* Infrastructure people are more like engineers than creative types, and they are often not very good communicators. Their personality tends to drive them toward analysis and the engineering of systems, where their focus is to make certain that data flows where it needs to go, whether that data is graphics, video, or data files (like spreadsheets). They tend to focus more on system designs, specs, and configurations, and are often not highly skilled in web and graphics, social media strategies, or A/V.

Tech Discipline	Typical Duties
Web & Graphic Design	• Creating websites (internal and external) • Graphic creation • Publication design, layout, and production
Audio/Video	• Operation and oversight of sound booth and related equipment • Video production (concept, storyboarding, production, editing)
Social Media	• Social media strategy formulation • Publishing and oversight of social media messaging • Operation and oversight of sound booth and related equipment • Video production (concept, storyboarding, production, editing)
Data Infrastructure	• Analysis and engineering of system to support data transmission & storage • Configuration and support of computers and devices

Figure 1: Typical IT Discipline Duties

Which Discipline Is Best-suited to Oversee IT?

I'm an infrastructure guy, so my perspective may be a bit biased. However, here is what I see at many churches:

- When non-infrastructure people oversee IT, the infrastructure requirements necessary to support the needs of the entire church staff are often underestimated. This is usually because of an inadequate understanding of infrastructure engineering and strategy and is evidenced by the tendency towards non-enterprise hardware specs (meaning that the hardware chosen is usually not what corporations would consider appropriate to support high reliability needs with minimal cost). Less art than science, the data infrastructure discipline is more about engineering than creativity or communication.

- The infrastructure discipline is the foundational basis for all data transfer needs, so it usually is the best discipline to lead the technology needs of the church. However, two areas that infrastructure people struggle with are communication and an over-restrictive approach to policies. These weaknesses can erode their relationships with staff and leadership (more on this in Chapter 2). Over-restrictive policies also often prompt church staff to find workarounds, which can create numerous other risks and challenges.

Regardless of which discipline is responsible to lead a church's IT Department, there are some things that can be done to improve it:

- If a non-infrastructure person leads the IT Department, it is important to have a good and trusted infrastructure person in the department or to have a relationship with a good and trusted infrastructure consultancy. The infrastructure perspective is essential to having a system that works well for all staff and provides optimal and reliable transfer of every kind of data needed by the entire church team.

- If the IT Department is led by an infrastructure person, that person should spend time getting to know the needs of the other three disciplines to make certain those needs are considered in the system design. They should also spend time with other church staff members and get to know their needs. In addition, the infrastructure person leading the department will need a champion at the church leadership level to help overcome the communication and policy challenges mentioned earlier.

- Because an infrastructure person needs someone at the leadership level to help overcome communication challenges and implement policy changes, IT infrastructure is usually best placed under the chief operating officer (COO) or chief financial officer (CFO) of the church. Infrastructure is more of an operations discipline than it is a program discipline.

Communication Is Key

Many data infrastructure people struggle with communication. Jason Powell, though himself a skilled communicator as IT Director for Granger Community Church near South Bend, Indiana, says it is helpful to have a great communication skills mentor. Granger's IT Department is included as a part of its Communications Department, another good way to overcome the communications challenges.

David Brown, Technology Director for Capital Christian Center in Sacramento, California, agrees that communication is key: "The chasm between vision and reality can be filled with jagged rocks. There has to be a bridge-builder who can communicate effectively in both worlds. The tech world can be too black-and-white or binary to communicate effectively to leadership. Being able to navigate necessary IT restrictions, while meeting the goals of leadership, will produce an outcome in which both sides are pleased."

CHAPTER 2

Who Is IT's Customer?

IIIIIIIIIIIIIII

Be a yardstick of quality. Some people aren't used to an environment where excellence is expected.

Steve Jobs [4]

IIIIIIIIIIIIIII

Many church team members complain that they feel like the IT Department restricts them. When a staff member expresses a need to the IT Department, the first answer is often, "No, you can't do that." This is even true when *leaders* express a need! IT restricts what can be done on church computers; for instance, IT won't allow software purchases, offsite data access, and more.

Some policies need to be in place to protect the church, but many IT policies are not a good fit for how church teams work. The challenge of finding a way to both protect the church and empower the team deserves an appropriate balance.

Why Is IT So Restrictive?

The answer is primarily an issue of influence. Church IT tends to be restrictive because of other IT environments that IT staff have worked in or been influenced by. IT in for-profit companies, academic insti-

---

4   Jeffrey Young, *Steve Jobs: The Journey is the Reward* (1988).

tutions, government agencies, and healthcare are all very restrictive, the latter two especially so. People working in church IT are heavily influenced by their frame of reference—or their consultants' frame of reference.

In non-church settings, IT security is often very high and employees are seen as a commodity. When a non-church IT Department determines that a policy is important, violating that policy is grounds for termination.

Churches are different. Employees are not a commodity. Each employee—or *team member*—is someone we care about and for whom Christ died. In churches, we try to apply grace and mercy. And that can sometimes create a passive-aggressive culture where everyone perceives IT policies as nothing more than ineffective speed bumps that are okay to bypass—everyone, that is, except the IT Department! This passive-aggressive culture can also frustrate those staff members who are uncomfortable with ignoring policies. The IT Department can end up feeling unappreciated.

While consulting for a megachurch, I saw the passive-aggressive dynamic in an advanced state:

- The IT Department was frustrated that the rest of the church staff seemed to ignore many IT policies in unforeseen and uncontrollable ways.

- Many on the church staff bragged to me about how they got around IT restrictions. Even top pastoral leaders in the church bragged about this. The executive pastor encouraged his team members to come up with ways to get past restrictive IT policies so they could get their job done!

- Some of the more compliant staff were frustrated on behalf of the IT Department and could not understand why everyone treated IT so disrespectfully.

Who Is IT's Customer?

One of the best ways to overcome this common conflict is for the IT Department to approach its role as though it is a for-profit business and every member of the church team is a customer.

Why does that help so much? A for-profit business knows it must meet its customers' needs effectively and in such a positive way that the customer will want to come back and give them more business. Anything less threatens a for-profit's very existence. Imagine the effect this underlying philosophy would have on most church IT Departments—and on the church teams they serve!

That means IT must not dictate what people may or may not do on the system, *except when it is necessary to protect the team members and/or the organization.* Restrictive policies that are not truly necessary have the same effect as crying wolf when no wolf is there: people stop paying attention to the warnings. Thus, any restrictive policy needs to be carefully scrutinized to determine how essential it is before it's put into place. Top church leadership can help determine the validity of the policy and require buy-in from the team. Leadership's response and decision to enact the policy will become the force behind it rather than the force coming from the IT Department.

Who Sets Policy?

IT teams often feel pressured to set appropriate IT policies to protect the organization, its team members, and its data. But that is *not* IT's responsibility. Rather, organizational leadership should set policy—with IT giving its input consultatively. IT's responsibility, in turn, focuses on implementing the policies leadership adopts.

For every IT policy need, IT should meet with organizational leaders and let them know that a policy is needed and why. IT needs to communicate effectively the need, the risks, the alternatives, and the costs.

For example, IT may want to implement something called two-factor authentication to improve security for systems and devices.

- If IT were to set that policy, those on the ministry team who didn't like the new policy (probably almost everyone!) would complain to leadership that IT is being too paranoid and heavy-handed.

- *If*, however, IT met with leadership and explained—in terms everyone could comfortably grasp—the reasons for two-factor authentication and the risks of not implementing it, and then let leadership make the decision, the team's angst would be with leadership, not with IT. Risk management is leadership's responsibility, so the decision is best made by organizational leaders!

This approach offers at least two benefits:

1. It helps end the tendency of some team members who try to get around IT's policies. These are *not IT's policies*—they're leadership's!

2. If leadership decides to not set a certain policy, and a problem later arises, IT will be there to help resolve the problem, but IT also will know it did its job when it properly advised organizational leaders.

We'll develop this concept further in Chapter 3.

Say "Yes" Whenever Possible

One year at a Church IT Network event, Clif Guy, Church of the Resurrection's IT Director in Leawood, Kansas, told us about his IT team's astonishing approach to requests: His church IT Department's policy is to say "yes" whenever possible. This approach is rare. But it is exactly the way IT should run in the church. The default posture always should be to say "yes!" That does not mean IT always says "yes" though. Sometimes the response really needs to be "no, and here's why." But having a "yes" default posture helps convey that IT is on the same team as the rest who are driven to fulfill their call.

Most church team members rarely understand the results of some IT-related decisions on overall productivity. IT needs to say "no" on occasion, but IT needs to say "no" so infrequently that when they do, the rest of the team will heed it.

Here Are a Couple of Practical Examples

1. Local Admin

One of the big debates at Church IT Network[5] events is over something called "local admin." When setting up a team member's computer, the option exists to give that team member administrative authority over their computer. Doing so does not affect the security rights the team member will have on the network and its data, but only on the computer they use day in and day out. Because it only affects their computer, and not the overall system, it is referred to as *local* admin rights.

---

5   Church IT Network, http://churchitnetwork.com.

About half of church IT people believe in giving everyone local admin rights, and the other half adamantly oppose it. I am a big proponent of giving all team members local admin rights unless one of them proves they just cannot safely handle that much authority. Giving everyone local admin rights has some valuable benefits:

- It allows team members to install printer drivers, flash drive drivers, and so on, without having to contact the IT Department.

- It allows the user to run application updates and patches without the IT Department's intervention.

- It dramatically reduces the number of support calls to the IT Department, lowering the time—and potentially, staff—needed to handle the load of resolving all those support calls.

- It builds "customer" satisfaction.

However, there is a risk to giving everyone local admin rights. For example, a team member has the ability to load malware on their system or delete a necessary operating system file. After using this strategy on thousands of church computers for many years, I have found the risk to be minimal.

If your church grants local admin rights to all team members, IT needs to engineer ways to protect and resolve issues that could arise because of local admin rights. However, doing so is a significantly lower load and cost than *not* giving local admin rights. Here are some ways for IT to protect the system:

- Fully back up the church's data daily, and keep at least three to four weeks of those backups in case a problem isn't noticed right away.

- Make hard drive images of local computers using an app like Clonezilla[6] so that, if necessary, reestablishing a computer's configuration can be quick and easy. This can be further simplified by buying similarly spec'd computers in bunches rather than individually, since all of the similar computers can be backed up by a single image.

If a team member repeatedly shows they cannot be trusted with local admin rights, change only that team member's rights instead of restricting everyone on the team. This helps IT build a level of "customer satisfaction" that is a blessing for every member of the team.

2. Convergence of IT and A/V

The Audio/Video discipline is converging with IT, and a common denominator—data infrastructure—is the reason why. A/V is beginning to depend more heavily on infrastructure technology—specifically using Internet Protocol (IP) over Ethernet cable for communication purposes. This forward shift in A/V communications offers big cost-savings potential. It also requires the two disciplines to work together, something IT team members are often reluctant to do.

IP over Ethernet

For more than three decades, IP over Ethernet cable, or even fiber-optic cable, has been IT's primary way of moving network data. Because of this, IT has a lot of experience on how to manage and maximize this medium of digital communication.

---

6   Clonezilla, https://clonezilla.org.

The problem, from the A/V perspective, is that IT is not willing to bring this experience to bear on A/V needs. The reason: A/V needs two certain things turned on to make its system perform correctly—things that IT has been told *not* to turn on:

- Internet Group Management Protocol (IGMP); and
- Jumbo frames (also known as "jumbos").

Over the decades, IT has learned that the more that is turned on in the network, the more complex and less reliable the network becomes. Normal data networks do not need IGMP or jumbos, so IT leaves them off.

But A/V needs IGMP and jumbos.

Given A/V's needs and IT's reluctance, A/V people conclude the A/V system must run through its own separate network, including separate cable and switches. A/V *needs* IGMP and jumbos, and since IT says "No," A/V *needs* budget funding for that separate network.

How Can These Two IT Disciplines Get Along?
Here's where IT can play a vital role in helping all members of the ministry team fulfill their calling—while also saving the ministry thousands of dollars.

The IT infrastructure can certainly handle the weight of the A/V team's needs. IT may need to do some research to learn how best to configure the system, but it boils down to adding a number of VLANs[7] running on higher-quality switches with things like IGMP and jumbos turned on. The IGMP and jumbos can be restricted to VLANs only used by

---

[7] VLANs are Virtual Local Area Networks—very common in data networking.

A/V. This restriction enables A/V to rely upon the IGMP and jumbos it needs to do video multicasts. It also allows IT to protect the network's reliability.

Jonathan Smith with Faith Ministries makes a great observation about this situation. If IT isn't willing to help A/V in this way, then A/V will have to buy a number of higher-end switches to meet its needs. It would be better to focus the funds A/V would unnecessarily spend to instead improve the reliability and quality provided by the better switches for all IP communications (which are needed all week by the entire team, not just A/V's needs six to eight hours per week) then to have to maintain physically separate or duplicated networks.

This Is Not Rocket Science!
Okay, maybe it is. But the point is that infrastructure folks divide digital communications over the same cable into multiple *virtual* networks all the time! With the right network equipment (enterprise-quality firewalls, switches, and cable that may already be in use at your church), different kinds of traffic over the same cable can coexist without interfering with each other. They can be set to act as though they are on separate cables, even though they're not.

That could mean that A/V doesn't need a separate network. And not requiring a separate A/V network can save a lot of money for implementation and for support over time.

The key is in the quality of the network hardware and its engineering.

Not All Network Equipment is Created Equal
Though I'll develop this topic further in Chapter 7, buying "right" really makes a difference. It's sort of like Goldilocks in *The Story of the Three Bears*! You can buy network hardware that is

- Underpowered (consumer specs),
- Overpowered (probably very expensive), or
- Just right! (effective mix of features and price)

The basis of A/V horror stories about sending A/V communications in a VLAN over the data network almost always points to inadequate hardware or engineering.

And this is where converging the two IT disciplines of A/V and infrastructure can prove wise. Your infrastructure team has been working with IP communications based on decades of experience and knowledge. IT needs to learn how to meet A/V's needs and then agree to help, and A/V needs to trust IT to meet their needs.

CHAPTER 3

Leading in an IT Vacuum

||||||||||||||||

If it wasn't hard, everyone would do it. It's
the hard that makes it great.

Tom Hanks [8]

||||||||||||||||

Church leadership makes decisions and sets direction for ministry programs, but usually without input or feedback from the IT Department.
Yet most decisions made today involve IT disciplines. Why does this
happen? How do we reasonably overcome it?

The Challenge

Ministers, boards, and committees meet regularly to talk through the
status of their church and identify strategic directions to increase
their effectiveness in their communities, among other things. These
strategic directions might be about seasonal programming (Easter
and Christmas, for example), group programming (young adults and
families, for example), or community event involvement (such as a
local parade). Each of these touch upon an IT discipline (graphics,
A/V, social media, and/or infrastructure).

Unfortunately, IT leaders often learn of these programming plans late
in the process.

---

[8]   *A League of Their Own,* Columbia Pictures (1992).

Common examples I have seen in churches include:

- "I just found out that we're supposed to provide WiFi to the entire congregation in one week for something the pastor will do during his message."

- "We're supposed to provide check-in stations in a new part of the building and add a new kiosk in the lobby, but we don't have the bandwidth or connections in that part of the building or a secure connection in the lobby. I only have four days to make this work."

- "We added a pastor to the staff today, and we need to give this new pastor a computer."

I also receive calls about A/V and website issues. The problem in these examples is that IT wasn't told early enough to adequately prepare; yet they are responsible for making it work! And the bulletin is already printed, so there's no way to adjust the schedule to allow for good preparation!

Very few churches and ministries include someone responsible for IT in the discussions and decisions for programming. Many churches see IT as operations overhead, so IT is not typically represented in those planning meetings.

The Consequences

Two common consequences of not having IT involved early enough in the planning process are:

1. Programming decisions are beyond the current ability of the church's IT disciplines to fulfill without expanding their hard-

ware, software, or talent. This is not inherently negative, but it can be if the cost is higher than leadership anticipated.

An example is a decision to add financial transaction terminals to the campus (giving kiosks, credit card terminals, and so on). Even if credit and debit card numbers will not be maintained locally, transmitting these over the church's network and internet connection can trigger something called PCI Compliance, which can be very expensive depending on how the terminals are connected. Strategic implementation requires advance notice.

2. Expansion of IT hardware, software, or talent cannot be strategic if not given advance notice. I have seen many churches and ministries use hardware that is nowhere near "enterprise grade" quality. Instead, they have "consumer grade" solutions in place.

Consumer grade solutions often get implemented because IT is up against a tight deadline and has to look for something—*anything!*—available in a store immediately. In Chapter 7 on "Rightsizing Hardware," I discuss the basis of one of my firm's catchphrases: "If you can find it on a shelf in a store, you probably don't want it!" When under a very tight, last-minute deadline, on-the-shelf consumer grade solutions often offer the only hope of avoiding failure. The result is low-quality solutions, which often cost more than appropriate solutions if given the appropriate time to order. From there, the problem persists because instead of replacing lower quality solutions once the deadline passes, the church keeps the consumer-grade solutions in place. That often translates into long-term reliance on solutions that have higher support costs and poorer performance, and that lowers team productivity.

What Does Corporate America Do?

Larger companies often have a CXO position (this is a general reference to a top leadership level person where the X is a wildcard; **C**hief **E**xecutive **O**fficer - CEO, **C**hief **O**perations **O**fficer - COO, **C**hief **F**inancial **O**fficer - CFO, and so on) who is responsible for all things IT. Although many churches and ministries are smaller than those large companies, we can still learn from this approach.

Many medium and larger corporations have a Chief Information Officer (CIO) or Chief Technology Officer (CTO) that participates in leadership meetings and on boards. These individuals help shape decisions and decision-making processes so IT can get the right solutions in place to facilitate plans.

What is a Reasonable *Church* Solution?

Adding a CIO or CTO to church leadership teams isn't the solution. Churches are focused on reaching the lost for Christ, and want as much of their budgets as possible to go toward programming rather than overhead.

IT usually reports to the CFO or COO of a church. That person often has the title of church administrator, church business manager, or executive pastor. Regardless of the title at your church, the person in that position needs to represent IT in leadership meetings in the same way a CIO or CTO would. The problem is that church CFOs and COOs usually don't know a lot about IT. That's okay if IT is managed strategically. I recommend the following:

- If leadership meetings happen regularly (weekly or monthly, for example), the CFO or COO should also have a regularly scheduled meeting with the IT person who reports to them to talk about the plans and directions that are being discussed in the leadership meetings *immediately* following the leadership meetings.

- If these follow-up meetings happen right on the heels of the leadership meetings, the leadership planning discussion will be fresh in the mind of the CFO or COO. He or she can then get the IT person's input, and relate any concerns to leadership within an appropriate timeframe. This can help leadership adjust planning if needed, and it gives IT notice of what may be coming so that IT can research and plan accordingly.

This is not an IT power grab! Rather, these meetings will help leadership accomplish plans for less money and will give IT enough advance notice to strategically research the appropriate enterprise-class solutions necessary for upcoming plans.

SECTION TWO

Church IT Solutions

||||||||||||||

Computers allow us to squeeze the most out
of everything.

Buzz Aldrin [9]

||||||||||||||

---

[9] Buzz Aldrin Tells Moon Landing Story, *Red Carpet News TV* (Aug. 3, 2012),
http://redcarpetnewstv.com/buzz-aldrin-tells-moon-landing-story/.

CHAPTER 4

Selecting Solutions for the Wrong Reasons

|||||||||||||||

People say I make strange choices, but
they're not strange for me.

Johnny Depp [10]

|||||||||||||||

When deciding how to meet a specific need, churches frequently ask other churches about solutions they used to meet that specific need. Whether it's hardware, software, or a database (such as Church Management Software), churches like to ask other churches what they use and whether they're happy with the choice to use it. That kind of research is good in theory but may not be in practice. It can have some significant downsides.

The Quest to Be a Good Steward

Churches have IT budget constraints because they want as much of their budget as possible to go toward programming. So, the faster and more efficiently they can find operational solutions, the better. Right? Sometimes. Referrals from other churches can help us avoid mistakes, point us in directions that are good, or point us in directions that are bad.

---

[10]   Johnny Depp Fan Page, Facebook (July 12, 2012), https://www.facebook.com/The
JohnnyDeppPage/.

Referral Request Assumptions

When we ask other churches for referrals of IT solutions, we make certain assumptions that may or may not be true. These assumptions are worth discussing. Here are two of the most significant:

- *Assumption 1:* "We are nearly identical. The other church is almost identical to ours in the way we do ministry, the things we value and prioritize, who we target in fulfilling our mission, the way our staffs are structured and work, and the way we minister to our congregation. Our two churches are nearly identical in personality, style, target, and focus."

- *Assumption 2:* "The other church researched its choice well. The other church did its due diligence in searching out the best possible solution based on its personality, style, target, and focus; its search was objective and exhaustive, landing on the best solution. In asking another church's leaders what they recommend, we save time and energy by not duplicating their research."

Problems with These Assumptions

With the first assumption, it is unlikely the two churches are identical. Although many churches have similar goals of reaching the lost and helping them become true followers of Christ, the way each church accomplishes their goals is different. These differences are shaped by the personalities, education, skills, and gifting of the staffs. The mission of a church shapes it, affecting its strategies to reach people. The location, the surrounding community, and the physical layout of a church also shapes it. Each church has a unique personality, style, and culture—so unique, in fact, that it makes it unlikely that the two churches are identical.

That said, it is unlikely one church wants to do the exact same thing as the other. I frequently see this when churches are looking for a new ChMS (Church Management Software). When one church relies heavily on another church or individual's recommendation, the solution rarely lasts five years. The dissatisfaction is often expressed in statements like, "The software just doesn't match our church's ministry needs and style."

In the second assumption, the problem is that the referring church probably did *not* do an exhaustive search for the best solution to match their needs. Rather, they probably did the same thing you would like to do—call another church and ask them for a referral. If you trace the chain of referrals, you may find the first church that had chosen the solution many now are using because of their decision did so because of a discount made possible by a friend or a spouse, rather than the "best of class" solutions available. Even if that decision somehow worked out for the first church, it is unlikely the same solution will work for subsequent churches looking for guidance.

Ultimately, decisions made solely or based too heavily on the recommendation of another church are likely to fail.

A Better Way

The best method is to do an objective, exhaustive analysis using the unique needs of your church to decide what solution is best. However, this requires a significant investment of time, and someone to see it through.

The best way to determine your church's needs is through surveys and/or interviews with your team members most affected by the solution. The key to success is to do this phase of research without an agenda favoring any of the ministries at your church.

From there, all solutions should be reviewed to determine which one best matches your church's needs.

My method is a bit more *old school*. I interview each team member (sometimes in individual interviews and sometimes in focus group interviews). In each interview, I first establish the person's role so I understand that person's perspective. Then I ask a few questions:

- What software and hardware do you use in your job? (This helps identify how many silos of data exist.)

- What tasks does the system do for you now that you consider crucial? (This helps document tasks the new system must be able to do.)

- What does the system do that slows you down or gets in the way? (This helps document potential areas of improvement the team would like in their new solution.)

- How could the system serve you better?

- What else would you like the system to do for you?

You may notice I never ask what solution they wish they had! The interviews identify needs that must be met in search of the best solution.

I ask these questions verbally in interviews (rather than through a questionnaire) because some of the answers lead to follow-up questions that glean information I would otherwise never get. Then I compile a survey (customized and built on previous surveys—more than 30 pages long) to send to all ChMS providers to help determine which solutions can best meet the church's needs. I also send a modified copy to the team members so they can weight each item on the survey, with choices of unimportant, might be nice, important, essential, or no opinion. I multiply the numeric values of the results of both groups to get an objective score for the providers most likely to meet the church team members' needs well.

Once you have objectively identified the top three solutions, you and your team should schedule live demos or visit other churches using them. This step helps your team members determine whether the solutions are good to use the way they would want to use them.

By involving your larger church team in the process, you will also help overcome one of the chief complaints of church staff. According to Chuck Lawless,[11] staff members often feel excluded from decision-making processes, making them feel they have no voice—that their opinions do not matter.

Giving your team a voice in the process takes more time and energy, but it increases team buy-in, encourages team members that their opinions are valued, and gets everyone focused on the positive aspects of the selected solution.

Do Your Research. It's Worth the Effort!

Many times quick decisions are made because such-and-such church uses a particular solution. Checking with other churches can help shorten the list of preferred solution providers. It also may add some solutions to the list that you may not have been aware of! Don't make the decision solely based on those recommendations.

---

[11] Chuck Lawless, *12 Frequent Burdens of Church Staff,* Managing Your Church (March 24, 2015), http://ManagingYourChurch.com.

Still do the research with your staff (they will thank you!). Gather a list of criteria to use in the decision-making process, and still require live demos, or visit churches with the solution in place to see if it will fit your church's culture.

CHAPTER 5

Windows or macOS?

||||||||||||||

If you don't mind, it doesn't matter.

Anonymous [12]

||||||||||||||

Church leaders still debate whether to run the Windows operating system, the macOS operating system (which requires an Apple Mac)— or both. This debate has caused angst for decades. Let's address it.

We have researched the pros and cons of churches running only one or both systems many times over the years, and formed an opinion based on the compatibility of the Mac processors with other computers on a given church's network.

In the early days, Apple focused on Motorola PowerPC processors to drive its Macs. These processors didn't coexist well on networks using Intel x86 processors. We therefore recommended a church focus on one platform or the other, but not one mixing the two.

Then, in 2005, Steve Jobs shook up the computing world when he announced Apple was transitioning Macs to Intel x86 processors! When we refreshed our Mac research a couple of years after the

---

[12] Anonymous government researcher referenced in Statesville Record and Landmark, Statesville, N.C. 1968.

announcement, we concluded Macs finally worked well on Intel-based networks.

Because of these developments, we no longer believe a mixed-platform environment is a problem. Churches may use both Mac and Windows operating systems on the same network without compromising performance. Macs do tend to cost more, which can affect church budgets, but outside of that consideration, we see both platforms as equally good.

What Really Matters

Salaries and benefits paid to staff are the most expensive budget item for most churches, so the efficient productivity of each team member is crucial to the mission of the church.

If one staff member will be most efficient on a Windows computer, while another staff member will be most efficient on a Mac, churches should consider giving each one the platform they prefer. Doing so maximizes the value of the cost spent on their salary and benefit packages, and doing so maximizes the efficient fulfillment of the church's mission.

Sharing Files and Collaboration

Some church leaders wonder whether mixed platforms will create problems with sharing files and collaboration between staff members. Most software solutions today run on both platforms with only minor differences in their feature sets, so sharing files and collaboration can work well.

Are There Dangers?

Yes, there are! But with a little strategy, providing both platforms to your church team can be done safely.

- Mac enthusiasts strongly believe a few things, even though the facts say otherwise. Let's discuss four of the most commonly stated assertions about Macs:

1. *Macs are not more expensive.* They are. Just compare similar specs of both types of operating systems. Again, though, if someone will be more productive on a Mac, it may be worth the additional expense.

2. *Macs require less support.* This one is a little more complex to address. Because Mac users are often independent in their approaches to technology, they help each other, and this can lower the number of support issues your IT Department or vendor must address.

   However, hardware failures with Macs are at least as high as ones running Windows systems, and they often require making an appointment for face-to-face time with a Level 1 support person (cleverly branded as a "genius") at a local Apple store. This is far more costly than the next-day warranties of some other manufacturers (like Dell) who will have someone come to your church to fix the computer.

3. *Mac users often prefer "better" solutions.* That independent spirit I mentioned in the above point means that sometimes Mac users will prefer using apps that are different than—and incompatible with—those used by Windows users.

4. *Macs are safer from malware and more secure.* Totally false! The Mac OS is easier to hack in to than any other operating system.

Each of these four assertions can be managed and effectively addressed. Here's how:

1. Mitigate the higher cost of Macs by focusing on the efficiency and productivity gained by the staff members who prefer using Macs.

2. Look for a vendor in your area that is an authorized Mac repair vendor. The vendor may offer more personalized and convenient hardware support. If they're approved by Apple for performing warranty repairs, then warranty repairs will be covered as though they were directly handled through Apple—and non-warranty repairs may cost less!

3. Ask church leaders to develop and adopt a policy regarding which software programs the team should use. This will reduce—or even eliminate—the possibility of staff members trying to share incompatible files.

4. Require all Macs to run anti-malware software. I recommend ThirtySeven4 (ThirtySeven4.com). Mac users also should be reminded regularly to physically protect their Macs at all times, particularly if they are using MacBooks.

After completing our updated Mac research in 2007, I wrote an article[13] and mentioned some of the weaknesses of the platform like I did here. Mac enthusiasts came unglued! I got more email from that article than almost all others combined. So I wrote a follow-up article factually explaining each of the weaknesses mentioned in the first article. I didn't get even one email.

---

13 Nick Nicholaou, *Can I Get a Mac?*, MBS, Inc. (Jan. 1, 2008), http://mbsinc.com/can-i-get-a-mac.

After many years of using a Windows-based computer, I have used a Mac almost exclusively since 2007. The bottom line for church leaders is this: whether it is a Mac operating system or a Windows operating system, the two platforms are good network citizens. It's okay to let those on your team use whichever platform they will be most efficient on.

CHAPTER 6

Church Management Software (ChMS)

|||||||||||||||||

*What turns me on about the digital age,
what excites me personally, is that you have
closed the gap between dreaming and doing.*

Bono [14]

|||||||||||||||||

Using computers in churches is different from most settings. How IT Departments in churches serve their "customers" and some of the solutions churches use are also different.

In the mid-1980s, I did my first exhaustive study on the software used by churches to manage financial and non-financial data. At that time, there were 262 solutions available to help in these vital areas! I established some reasonable minimal criteria for review, and only 17 made it through that filter! That meant there were many inadequate solutions. Because there were so many to choose from, it was nearly impossible for a church to do a good and thorough analysis.

Since those early days of church computing, many solution providers have merged, consolidated, or gone out of business. Many new solutions have sprung up, too!

---

[14] Paul David Hewson (Bono), (2005) TED Conference.

We collectively refer to these solutions as ChMS solutions. Today there are about 75 viable solutions written for churches and marketed to help them in these areas.

Why ChMS Instead of More General Solutions?

The financial and non-financial needs of churches are unique and not easily met with non-ChMS solutions.

In the financial area:

- Church accounting systems need to track various income and expense transactions, many of which close to different "capital"-equivalent accounts that are restricted (temporarily or permanently) or unrestricted. This is an accounting issue that sets church accounting needs apart from most other organizations:

  - Income and expense accounts close to a capital account—in companies it might be retained earnings; in churches it is a fund balance, also referred to as a net asset.

  - The unique aspect of nonprofit accounting is that income and expense accounts tied to various purposes and funds (like the missionary fund, the building fund, and so on) need to close to those various fund balance accounts and produce an available balance of how much is in each fund being tracked.

    This helps fulfill one of the unique responsibilities churches have in their accounting systems, which, according to ECFA President Dan Busby, is "using the gifts within the limits of the donor's restrictions. To accomplish this, churches must have accounting systems which not only track restricted gifts in the donor management system, but also track the expenditure of the funds and unused funds (temporarily restricted net assets)."[15]

- Many churches keep their books on a "cash basis" or "modified cash basis," with only a small percentage of churches on the "accrual basis." A ChMS solution needs to accommodate all three. (Modified cash is a mixture of the cash and accrual methods in which some items, accounts payable, for example, are managed on a cash basis.)

- There are unique aspects to managing payroll in churches. For example, ministers' income may or may not be subject to income tax withholding. The housing allowance portion of their income needs to be tracked as federally non-taxable, and none of their income is subject to FICA withholding.

In the non-financial area:

- Churches track all kinds of demographic and contact information. That's not uncommon among Customer Relationship Management (CRM) solutions. What makes it much more complex in churches are contributions, attendance, security check-in and check-out for children's ministries, event registration, life events, and the family/extended-family relationships that need to be tracked.

- An important database function in many churches is the ability to securely check children in and out for children's ministry

---

15   Dan Busby, Four Accounting Challenges for Churches, ECFA (2015), www.ecfa. church/content/four-accounting-challenges-for-churches-church.

events, such as Sunday school. In addition to the checking in and out process, churches need to track allergies, restraining orders, restricted access, and many other pieces of data that keep children safe—and help parents feel their children are safe.

- Tracking attendance helps identify those who may need some follow-up and encouragement

- Tracking contributions and pledges is essential. This feature is normally considered a ChMS non-financial feature because many solution providers do not offer their own accounting solution, but all need to offer contributions tracking. There are specific legal requirements that allow contributors to write-off their contributions at tax time that these systems must satisfy.

Why Not Create Your Own Software Solution?

Many churches and ministries have gone the route of creating their own software solution. It rarely works for these reasons:

- *It will never be completed.* The process of creating your own software solution begins with gathering a list of needs, and then creating the software solution to meet those needs. After writing it, the testing begins, followed by fixes. Then more testing happens, and then, hopefully, it is released for use. To get to a release date takes a lot of time, energy, and focus. As users begin to use the new custom solution, the list of needs will expand beyond the original list. Then more work begins to release version 2, version 3, and so on. Buying a full-featured ChMS means that most of what the church team wants will be included because of the solution provider's experience with so many churches. Implementation also will happen much faster in comparison.

- *It will be difficult to support.* Every software solution requires support, which requires someone to support it. Then, when underlying operating system (OS) updates are released (like Windows or macOS), the solution needs to be tested and modified based on those new OS requirements. In addition, we all eventually move on, either geographically or because our life's time has ended. When that happens, the church will need to find someone who can take responsibility for the custom solution, further develop it, and support it. Finally, because of the time and work involved, it's unlikely the process will be well-documented, meaning subsequent developers and staff members will struggle using it.

- *It will be **very** expensive.* The amount of time spent to develop, implement, support, and upgrade the solution will be very expensive. Add to that the cost of lost staff productivity while the solution is tested and enhanced. It is a very expensive proposition; one I very rarely recommend.

I write an annual article that lists the current providers of ChMS solutions. It is published in numerous journals and available on many websites, including my firm's website.[16]

Reasonable Expectations

Churches and ministries often ask me to help them look for a new ChMS database and/or accounting system. During those conversations, I talk through what their team can expect from whatever new solution they choose. Most people don't realize what "there is no perfect solution" truly means. The very best anyone can expect is an 80- to 85-percent match with the expectations and needs of any

---

[16]   MBS, Inc., https://www.mbsinc.com/church-donor-management-software-chms/.

church or ministry. Stated from the other side of that equation, the lowest number of missed expectations they can hope for is about 15 percent to 20 percent.

If a church already has a top-tier solution, the process of searching for and transitioning to a new solution may be nothing more than trading one 20-percent set of missed expectations for a different set of 20-percent missed expectations. If that's true, then that church may be better off exploring other ways to overcome their dissatisfaction before starting the transition journey. I'll address this further in Chapter 13.

Data Normalization

In nearly every ChMS consultation, we have to tell the church that, based on the old adage "garbage in/garbage out,"[17] its data must be cleaned up first before importing the data into a new ChMS database. The industry term for this process is "data normalization."

Data normalization is needed to create reliable, efficient uses of the ChMS. It becomes a need because a church team either fails to establish a set of standards before any data gets entered—or fails to train people on the standards set, including new hires and volunteers. Without correction, the problem only grows larger.

Here's a common scenario that illustrates this problem:

> One existing data point for the children's ministry may be the name of the school each child attends. Children's ministry staff and volunteers complain about the unpredictable results they receive whenever they search for all of the kids from a particular elementary

---

[17]   Also referred to as "GIGO."

school. The cause? Different team members have entered varied spellings for each school, either because no standard was set or there wasn't training with an established standard. For instance, Abraham Lincoln Elementary School may have been entered into the ChMS as:

- Abraham Lincoln Elementary School
- Abe Lincoln Elementary
- Abe Lincoln
- ALE

That doesn't even include misspellings! There's no way to get a predictable list when searching for a data point that is not normalized.

The solution to fix this is very tedious. But it is necessary. Someone needs to look for every record with this data point and normalize it to the standard the church wants to use.

Think of how many different data points your church has in its database—the task of normalizing all of them seems insurmountable! But a normalized database is essential. It will produce better, more efficient results with the ChMS in the long run. Such a project offers a terrific opportunity to use volunteers, so contemplate ways to recruit and oversee them to do it.

CHAPTER 7

Rightsizing Hardware

||||||||||||||||

It is far more important to be able to hit the
target than it is to haggle over who makes a
weapon or who pulls a trigger.

Dwight D. Eisenhower [18]

||||||||||||||||

One of the most common mistakes churches and ministries make is related to the hardware they buy. I can say this objectively because my firm does not sell or profit from the hardware or software our clients purchase. Hardware and software sales have never been in our game plan.

The mistake manifests itself three ways:

1. Incredible overspending on highly sophisticated hardware the church will never take advantage of (overbuying),
2. Buying consumer grade hardware that doesn't work very well in a corporate network setting (underbuying), and
3. Buying hardware built locally.

---

[18]   President Dwight Eisenhower, Address to the American Society of Newspaper Editors and the International Press Institute, (April 17, 1958).

In each of these mistakes, the church usually spends more on its purchases than necessary, either in outright purchase costs or in higher support costs and lost staff productivity.

Our firm works hard to stay neutral with hardware, software, and platforms so we can effectively evaluate the options in the marketplace and make appropriate recommendations to our clients. This chapter reflects that neutrality.

Overbuying

Most vendors do not understand the needs of churches, and thus have a difficult time making appropriate recommendations. Some overestimate the church's needs, recommending hardware with sophisticated features the church will never use.

Overbuying is often the result of one of three things:

1. *Buying based on possible future needs.* Many churches think somewhat aggressively when expressing their growing technology needs. But if those anticipated needs don't materialize for three or four years, the result will be overbuying.

2. *Recommendations based on limited understanding.* Churches are unique in their hardware needs. If the church trusts someone's 'counsel' who has limited perspective (someone whose IT expertise is focused in another industry), the result will often be overbuying.

3. *Vendor recommendations that affect the vendor's profit.* My firm has been to many churches that previously used IT vendors who sold them hardware based on what they made, sold, or had in stock, but the hardware didn't come close to appropri-

ately meeting the church's needs. It could be because a member of the congregation worked for the company selling the hardware. In many cases, my firm has concluded the overbuying by a church usually is caused by a vendor trying to get a larger sale, rather than trying to meet a church's specific need.

The most common example of overbuying occurs with Cisco firewalls and switches. These powerful, feature-rich solutions can almost definitely meet any church's needs. In fact, they significantly *exceed* the needs of most churches! The problem is that the features of Cisco firewalls and switches require a deep understanding of IT communication technology, and so their configuration and maintenance require a Cisco-certified engineer. That is expensive! And those higher-end features rarely benefit churches and ministries.

A church recently needed a local area network (LAN) revamp because its current configuration wasn't meeting its needs. When looking at their server configuration, my firm discovered it surpassed many servers found in high-end datacenters! The church spent more than twice what it needed on that server, and the church would never come close to taking advantage of its huge processor, random-access memory (RAM), and storage capacities.

Underbuying

Many churches and ministries mistakenly buy their computers from big-box retailers, electronics stores, or via internet searches. Many IT professionals have a saying in common: *If you can find what you need on a shelf in a store, you probably don't want it.* That goes for computers, printers, switches, and more—almost anything IT.

There are differences between enterprise-spec systems and consumer-grade systems. Here are a couple that may not be readily apparent:

- The engineering and match-up of components are at a higher level in enterprise systems than are usually found in consumer-grade systems. What many don't realize is that most computer components for both specs (consumer and enterprise) are manufactured on the same assembly line or process. The components are tested after being manufactured, and depending on how they score in testing, their test (or performance results) will determine their model number and associated cost. Thus, similar-looking components can be in both systems, but they will perform very differently over time. Enterprise-spec systems usually include higher-rated components, and have a higher level of research and development (R&D) invested in them by the company whose name is on the product (Dell, HP, and so on).

- Consumer-grade computers usually have a lot of trialware (software you get to try before you buy, but probably don't want). Companies offer trialware to try to influence you to buy their software after trying it. This approach helps underwrite the cost of the computer, which lowers its purchase price. Trialware usually means a less efficient user experience, and less-efficient user experiences translate to wasted time—and sometimes higher support costs.

  Another problem with trialware is that it often doesn't uninstall completely. The little bits and pieces left behind can sometimes be the cause of problems that users later encounter.

Underbuying is often the result of having to buy something fast because there wasn't a strategy in place to anticipate needs and allow purchases to be planned. Planned purchases usually mean better stewardship because they allow time for ordering enterprise-spec systems at the lowest possible cost. Enterprise-spec systems don't necessarily cost a lot more; they're just better in an enterprise (non-consumer) environment where systems are networked.

Buying Locally Built Systems

In the early days of personal computers, many people thought buying locally built computers was best. They thought the support would be better since they were built nearby. Maybe in the 1980s that was sometimes true, but more often *locally built systems need more support* because they do not have the benefit of the level of R&D a larger company, like Dell or HP, could invest in them. Even consumer-class systems have some R&D. But locally built systems are only assembled. A local shop may do its best to buy great components, but local shops have limited opportunity or capability to test how each of those components work together. Local shops certainly do not have the buying power to request manufacturer firmware changes to components that would improve the way their component interacts with other selected components.

Surprisingly, some churches still buy locally built systems! There is no way a local shop can compete with the quality, reliability, and support of a well-engineered system. And another surprise: locally built systems almost always cost more, not less!

So buy right! Buy enterprise systems for your church or ministry. You will save in the end.

Discovering What to Buy

Finding out what is best to buy can be challenging. Stores can't help you buy enterprise-spec hardware, so where can you turn?

The best answer is to find a vendor with expertise in configuring, engineering, and supporting enterprise networks—preferably in church and ministry settings. At the end of Chapter 15, I list a few resources that can help, but that list is not by any means complete.

There are also some association resources that can help you find someone that can help:

- The Church Network (thechurchnetwork.com)
- Church IT Network (churchitnetwork.com)
- Christian Leadership Alliance (christianleadershipalliance.org)
- Your denominational, movement, or association office.

CHAPTER 8

Virtual Computers

IIIIIIIIIIIIII

It's better to be a fake somebody than a real
nobody.

Matt Damon [19]

IIIIIIIIIIIIII

In the late 1990s, a technology was introduced into modern computing that existed previously only on large mainframe and midrange
computers. That technology, called *virtualization*, made it possible
for a computer or server to concurrently run multiple computers—
on one device!

At first, I was skeptical. How would it affect performance and reliability? And why would anyone want to do such a thing?

Many churches ask the same questions—if they are even aware of
this technology. At national and regional conferences, when I ask for
a show of hands, rarely do even 25 percent of church leaders indicate
they have virtualized servers.

This technology can save churches a lot of money, improve network
reliability, and improve network administration. And it's free! Well,
free for most churches, anyway—more on that in a bit.

---

19   *The Talented Mr. Ripley,* Miramax Films (1999).

How Does Virtualization Work?

Virtualization requires an app called a *hypervisor*, which functions like a shim or wedge between the bare hardware and the operating system (like Windows, macOS, or Linux). Rather than installing the OS directly onto the computer or server, the hypervisor is installed first. Once it is installed, a wizard then helps you install as many virtual computers onto the physical computer or server as it has resources (processors, RAM, storage, and so on) to host! Thus, the physical computer is often referred to as a host. To help explain how this works, the steps to creating a host and the computers and servers that will run on it are:

1. Install the hypervisor on a computer before installing any other operating systems (the hard drive should be empty when installing it).

2. Use the hypervisor's wizard, or menu, to say you want to create a virtual computer or server. Answer the hypervisor's questions about:

   a. What operating system you'll install on the virtual machine.
   b. How many processors you want the virtual system to have.
   c. How much RAM you want the virtual system to have.
   d. How much storage (hard drive size) you want the virtual system to have.

3. The hypervisor then takes a few minutes to create the virtual computer as you've spec'd it *logically* (vs *physically*). Once it's done, it will tell you to insert the OS installation media (like

inserting a DVD or pointing to an ISO file[20]). From that point forward, it looks like you're doing a normal OS installation, except that it's running in a window because it is a *virtual* computer!

Depending on the host's physical resources, you can install many virtual computers and servers. In my firm's datacenter, we run dozens on a single host!

Why Would You Want a Virtual Computer?

Physical computers and servers cost a lot of money. The surprising thing about them, though, is that for the most part, their physical resources go largely unused. For instance, if you were to monitor the processor's activity level in a server after it starts up, you'd find that it rarely goes above 10 percent utilization, except during the computer's start-up and shut-down. The processor is the most expensive component in the machine, and yet most of the time it is idle! The same is true for many other resources. Virtualization helps maximize the return on investment made when purchasing that machine.

When I first began working with virtual servers and computers, I was skeptical a virtual server could deliver the high degree of reliability churches need. I learned a properly configured one could.

One of the reasons virtualization improves reliability is that the best way to set up network servers is to do so with each major separate network service having its own server. So, an email server should run on its own server, as should a database server, file server, endpoint server, and so on. That means the best reliability requires many servers. That strategy would be out of reach for most church budgets were it not for virtualization.

---

20 An ISO file is an image of a CD or DVD that can be mounted logically just as though it was physical media. You can also burn an ISO file to optical media and run it that way.

With virtualization, you can have a couple of physical servers—or hosts (we call them vh1, vh2, and so on, for virtual host 1, virtual host 2, and

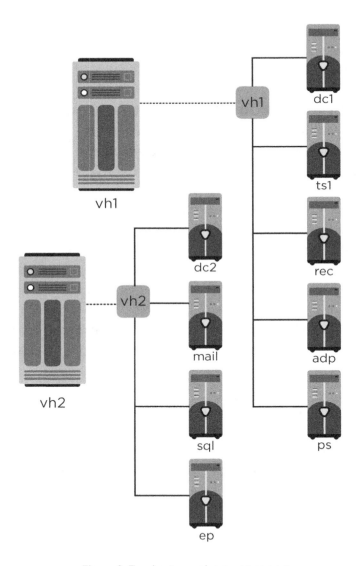

Figure 2: Two hosts running seven servers

so on)—provide the resources for many virtual servers (see Figure 2). That amounts to large savings—with improved reliability. A win-win!

Virtualization is what powers the cloud! All of those cloud solution providers are running nearly all of their servers as virtual servers. Doing so saves money on hardware and substantially improves reliability.

Brands and Costs of Hypervisors

There are three main players in the hypervisor marketplace: VMware's vSphere Hypervisor, Microsoft's Hyper-V, and Citrix's XenServer. All three are free for most churches.

VMware pioneered the technology, and its solution, vSphere, is currently the most mature, powerful, and the easiest to use. Hyper-V is growing in its abilities, but vSphere still has the edge, which is why I recommend it.

Since hypervisors are free for most churches, what is the business model behind them? These companies make their income through tools and features that only large organizations need. The best way to tell if your church needs those features is to determine whether or not your organization uses a SAN (Storage Area Network) on the network. SANs are *very* expensive devices, usually costing more than $25,000. If you have a SAN, you know it because of the high cost, and the relatively small cost of the hypervisor features you would want would be a slam-dunk decision to purchase.

Most churches do not have a SAN. That means the basic set of features included in the free hypervisor should take care of your needs!

The Bottom Line

The bottom line on virtualization for any church with one or more on-site servers is that if your church hasn't already, it most likely should be taking advantage of the power and reliability virtualization can add to your network. The price tag is certainly no barrier for doing so!

CHAPTER 9

Software Charity Licensing

||||||||||||||||

I was called to do this, and when you are
called to do something you don't give up. If
you believe in something strongly enough,
you continue to push until you find a way to
make it work.

Chris Booth [21]

||||||||||||||||

In the early 1990s, Chris Booth and I (and probably others, too) independently lobbied solution providers to offer licensing discounts to churches similar to those available to academic organizations and government agencies. The first large provider to agree to my request was Novell, a company that pioneered the software that made standardized local area networks possible. Then, mostly due to Chris' efforts, the second was WordPerfect, the pioneer for word processing software. Microsoft was third. (Microsoft eventually won both of those software categories due to its code development focus and market strategy.)

21   L. Roberts, A Higher Calling: Chris Booth gave up corporate life to bring bargain high-tech supplies, services to nonprofit organizations, *The Journal Times* (Nov. 28, 2008), https://journaltimes.com/lifestyles/faith-and-values/religion/a-higher-calling-chris-booth-gave-up-corporate-life-to/article_e2d23fbf-310c-515c-83fa-db7e4124c478.html.

Today, many solution providers offer discounted charity licensing discounts at, or near to, academic licensing discounts. Surprisingly, I still meet many in ministry that are unaware of these terrific discounts! Thus, they unnecessarily overspend on software.

Why Are Charity Discounts Offered?

Discounts are a great way for solution providers to offer philanthropic assistance to organizations that help society, but there is also a solid business case for doing so!

Board members and many other volunteers run churches and ministries. Many of those are decision makers or decision influencers in their paid jobs. Their hearts are definitely tied to helping the churches they serve to be effective.

Those same volunteers and board members, often in an effort to increase effectiveness at a reasonable cost for church computing, end up championing the same solutions at their paid jobs. Discounts to churches and ministries make for very inexpensive marketing for the solution providers!

Lee Iacocca, an auto industry leader who helped run Ford Motor Company, was the father of the Mustang, and the man who eventually turned Chrysler around from near bankruptcy, used a similar strategy. It was one of his many successes. In his autobiography,[22] he said the challenge in the auto industry was to find new ways to get folks to test drive their cars. When he realized that in the car rental industry people were actually *paying* to test drive cars, he made selling new cars at a low price to rental car companies a priority that translated into many test drives!

---

[22]   Lee Iacocca, *Iacocca: An Autobiography* (1984).

Where Can You Get Charity License Pricing?

Many sellers of software have the ability to sell charity licenses. The key is to ask your software solution seller to make certain they are using charity-licensing SKUs when selling you software. If you're not certain that you are being offered true charity licensing, check with the solution provider (Microsoft, VMware, and so on). If a solution you want to use doesn't offer charity-licensing discounts, ask them if they'd be willing to extend their academic licensing discount to your organization. Really, it is in their best interest to do so. Don't pay full retail because doing so is usually not necessary for a charity.

Charity Licensing Pitfalls

A few companies are changing the way they offer charity-licensing agreements, and it involves a danger for many churches and ministries. These solution providers are including specific restrictions in the charity license that sometimes conflict with the doctrine of many churches and ministries. Avoiding those licensing agreements may be in your church's best interest.

The two most prominent solution providers including these restrictions are Google and Microsoft. Both do it exclusively with their online solution charity-licensing agreements, but—interestingly—not with their academic licensing agreements. In Microsoft's case, it also is not doing this with its volume license charity-licensing agreements.

In the charity-licensing agreement for Google's G-Suite, charities are required to certify they do not discriminate in hiring or in employment practices related to the lesbian, gay, bisexual, and transgender (LGBT) community in any way. Microsoft's Office 365 charity license is similar, though we recently had success in getting them to add a statement and a FAQ explaining that churches and religious organizations may not be required to adhere to their certification requirements based on state and federal laws that govern churches and religious organizations and allow certain types of discrimination.

So Microsoft is making room for churches and ministries in their license agreements. Google, however, is not.

This is not a legal issue (though it could impact a legal proceeding); it is a mechanism Google is using to filter which organizations they want to donate their software to. Falsely certifying that an organization does not discriminate in its employment practices regarding LGBT issues, then, is taking from Google what they do not want to give.

In raising this concern, I am not taking the position that this should or should not be an issue. Christian churches and ministries love individuals in the LGBT communities. They want to serve them by introducing them to Christ and helping them grow in their relationship with him—a value-changing relationship! However, for many organizations, the employment practices requirement in the agreements pose a problem. It's important for churches and ministries to be aware of these restrictions. Just as I was involved in lobbying for charity discounts so many years ago, I am hoping to help remove this language from these licenses.

Don't Be Afraid of Hearing "No"

Many years ago I read a book on negotiating that said most people don't ask for concessions when they have an opportunity to negotiate because they're afraid of a "no" response. That affected me, and I began asking for concessions more often than I did previously. Sometimes I get the "no" response, but many times, I get a "yes" if the request is reasonable. So, if your software solution provider does not offer charity-licensing discounts yet, ask for it. The worst the provider can say is "no"!

CHAPTER 10

Making WiFi Work

ılıllıllıllıllı

Whenever you find yourself on the side of
the majority, it is time to reform.

Mark Twain [23]

ılıllıllıllıllı

Many churches today broadcast WiFi on their campus for the convenience of staff and guests. WiFi seems to behave mysteriously, though, and only a small percentage are completely pleased with how their WiFi works. There are reasons for it (largely hardware spec related), and there are strategies that every church would be wise to have in place to protect the church and to protect those who use its WiFi.

Can WiFi Be Reliable?

The short answer is *yes*, but the long answer is *yes, if you understand how it works and engineer accordingly*. The problems many experience with their WiFi campus deployments are fairly predictable, and easily avoided.

The most common WiFi complaints include:

- *People can't get a connection.* This is most often a hardware spec problem. The cause is usually from using consumer-spec WiFi

---

[23] Mark Twain, *Mark Twain at Large* (1878).

access points (WAPs), which directly relates to the discussion in the Underbuying section of Chapter 7 (see page 61). The WAPs you can find on a shelf and buy usually have a limit of about 25 connections. Some think that buying a bunch of them will overcome that limitation, but it doesn't.

• *The WiFi is too slow and devices drop their connection.* WAPs broadcast their signal over channels that, if not managed, bleed over and interfere with each other. Also, few routers or firewalls have the appropriate specs to accommodate the large burst of internet traffic that happens during church services and programs.

When engineering and configuring WiFi for church service guests, you are, in effect, establishing WiFi the same as you would for a small (or maybe not-so-small) convention center! And just as it would be true for a convention center, most of the time, the use of this resource is low—until a crowd shows up! That's when the WiFi must be set up appropriately to meet the needs of that crowd.

• *People can access content we don't want them accessing.* WAPs that are simply plugged into church network switches or routers can allow access to the internal network systems (like servers and printers) and to inappropriate websites. They need to be managed by a firewall or controller, something few off-the shelf WAPs can accommodate.

Hardware

I mentioned that off-the-shelf WAPs have a limit of about 25 connections that can connect to them at a time. Buying ten of them does not increase the capacity to 250 as you'd anticipate. The problem is that their hardware doesn't have the feature set necessary to allow them to work together. Instead, they conflict with each other and even interfere with each other.

My firm and I learned this the hard way. We found the answer was to recommend WAPs designed to operate in a commercial environment—in a convention center. We prefer Ruckus WAPs. Ruckus has some WAPs that can accommodate 500 or more concurrent connections and can coordinate with other WAPs when there are many deployed on a campus!

That is different than "mesh" technology, which doesn't handle the larger requirements of church guest WiFi needs well.

The next piece of the solution is the firewall. In Chapter 19, I explain why we recommend SonicWALL firewalls. The key to a good WiFi system is that the firewall needs to be able to handle the volume of internet traffic that happens during church services and programs. As I mentioned, few off-the-shelf units have what's needed.

The firewall also helps protect those connected to the church's WiFi from websites that have inappropriate content. This is essential—especially if children might be connecting to the internet.

Configuration

When you search for a WiFi signal with a device you'd like to connect (smartphone, tablet, computer, etc), you see a listing of names. Those WiFi signal names are Service Set Identifiers, or SSIDs. We typically configure three SSIDs for churches. These are managed in the firewall and are an important part of a good WiFi strategy.

The three SSIDs we usually configure for churches are:

1. *Guest.* This SSID only has access to the internet, and that access is filtered in both directions (incoming and outgoing) to prevent adult-oriented website access.

2. *Lay.* This SSID is similar to the Guest SSID, but it is password protected and has protected bandwidth to accommodate lay leaders who need to access YouTube or other similar streaming content while teaching a class. It might also include access to a printer to accommodate the need to print speaker notes or handouts.

3. *Staff.* This SSID is password protected and may even be hidden so that only those who need it know it exists! It is only for church staff and includes access to the internet and to network servers and devices.

WiFi Security

It is wise and prudent for churches to protect access to their WiFi system. The best recommendation is to password protect each SSID.

A church in Missouri learned the hard way that open and unprotected WiFi can cause significant problems. The church's WiFi was not protected with a password, and it ran 24/7. Someone was driving into their parking lot after hours, connecting to their WiFi from the parking lot, and distributing child pornography. When the FBI investigated, two things happened that caused the church problems:

1. The FBI confiscated the church's computers—*all* of them, including the servers! The FBI confiscated them because it is required to do a forensic examination to determine if any were involved in the distribution of child pornography. The church was without its computers for months, which would cause

problems for any church due to dependencies on computers for operations, study prep, and so on.

2. The story hit the news in a big way—television and newspapers. A headline in one newspaper was "Child porn investigation focused on [the church name]." A television news report was titled "Child porn linked to church IP address." You can imagine how this bad press impacted the church, and how long it would take to recover from the impact.

Most churches, in the name of being a *welcoming church*, don't want to password protect their guest WiFi. For churches who make that choice, we recommend—at a minimum—they turn off their SSIDs that are not password protected when no church service or program is running. That's only possible (without manually unplugging all WAPs) if the church is running an enterprise-class solution like the one my firm recommends (SonicWALL firewall with Ruckus WAPs). The SonicWALL can turn the guest WiFi on and off based on a set schedule that the IT manager can override if/when needed.

Taking Security a Step Further

While considering WiFi security, let me mention a vulnerability I see at many organizations (not just churches): default passwords still in effect for devices. This applies to WAPs, but it applies to other IT devices, too. A good practice is to always replace the default password on *any* IT device.

Gary Messmer, my firm's lead engineer, was visiting an auto dealership for routine car maintenance. While sitting in their waiting room, he looked to see if there was a WiFi signal (SSID) he could use. He found one, but it was password-protected. The SSID was named the default name with the WAP model assigned by the WAP's consumer-class manufacturer! Being familiar with those devices, he decided to try the default password. He was in! He connected to the dealership's database and pulled up someone's record, walked over to the service manager, and while showing him his computer screen asked, "Is this your dealership database?" The service manager was shocked!

In Chapter 19, I discuss why churches need to be proactive about managing their IT security. All data is vulnerable, but in the church, we need to make certain we are doing our due diligence to protect our data and the information that could hurt someone if it were inappropriately accessed.

CHAPTER 11

VoIP vs. Traditional Phone Systems

IIIIIIIIIIIIIIII

The overall point is that new technology will not necessarily replace old technology, but it will date it. By definition, eventually, it will replace it.

Steve Jobs [24]

IIIIIIIIIIIIIIII

Several years ago, I decided my firm needed a new phone system. Our system at that time was a peer-to-peer system, and it was significantly limited.

Our Challenge

When looking at our options, I was concerned with the prices normally associated with new phone systems. Typical PBX phone systems (Private Branch Exchange, typified by having an operator or receptionist) can cost tens of thousands of dollars!

To serve churches and ministries well, my firm runs on a very thin margin, so I didn't want to spend unnecessarily. I decided to look for something less traditional that wouldn't cost as much. Most churches

---

[24] Steve Jobs, Steve Jobs: His own words and wisdom, (2011).

also operate on thin margins, so I realized that the fruit of our quest might be useful to churches as well.

Initially, the solution to my quest seemed to be VoIP (Voice Over Internet Protocol), but even many of those systems cost more than $10,000. At a Church IT Network event I attended around that time, a number of attendees talked about a free PBX server that could run as a virtual server. I was leery because "free" is often more expensive than it's really worth. But considering the expense of the alternative, I decided to research this further and give it a try.

There are two aspects to VoIP:

1. Connecting your building to the world telephone system via VoIP technology vs. standard phone line technology (in Figure 3, this is referring to how the server in the bottom-right corner of the church connects to the worldwide telephone system).

   - This is what most people think of when they think of a VoIP system.

   - Standard phone lines are costly, and VoIP connections can save you significant money!

   - The vendor we prefer for VoIP connections is Bandwidth.[25] This vendor provides its Session Initiation Protocol (SIP) trunks to churches for a significant discount!

---

[25] Bandwidth, http://bandwidth.com.

– Metered lines (no free long distance or toll calls) for $15 per month per trunk. Long distance and toll calls bill at less than 2 cents per minute.

– Unmetered lines (long distance and toll calls included) for $22.50 per month.

I recommend churches get the metered lines since it would take more than 6 hours per month per trunk to get the metered cost up to the unmetered cost.

VoIP SIP trunks save churches money every month!

2. The internal corporate phone system, known as a PBX, that connects church team members via extensions. (In Figure 3 below, this refers to all of the phones and the computer they

Figure 3: Illustration of VoIP Components

connect to inside the church.) The PBX is figuratively the server in the bottom-right corner of the church.

PBX Technology

The PBX concept and its technology is very mature (dating back to the 1800s!), and there now are a number of free, open-source PBXes available that are solid. While researching the options, I found that most recommended the same one mentioned at the Church IT Network event, so I decided to test it to see if it was as good as suggested.

My firm downloaded a solution called Asterisk and configured it as a virtual server on one of our hosts. We found it solid but challenging. A colleague who works on VoIP PBX systems recommended we switch to a version of the same solution called FreePBX. He said it was based on Asterisk, but with more features and a better graphical user interface (GUI). We switched and haven't looked back!

That Got Us Thinking...

One of my firm's goals is to help Christian churches and ministries focus as much of their budget as possible on their ministry programs. Since they could save a lot of money by making their next PBX upgrade a FreePBX server, my firm needed to help them move in that direction! We started helping churches and ministries implement FreePBX phone systems because our conclusion agreed with the initial research: PBX solutions are a very mature technology, and spending tens of thousands of dollars on a phone system just isn't as necessary today as it was in the late 1900s!

Options Are The Biggest Challenge!

Designing a FreePBX phone system can be overwhelming because the technology is so capable. It has a lot of options. Here are some to consider:

- *Physical Handsets or Softphones with Headsets?*

  - One option is to eliminate physical handsets (the traditional telephones that sit on a desk) and instead use softphones. Softphones are apps that run on computers, tablets, and smartphones. Some of the benefits include:

    - *More desk space for other things.* This is similar to how no longer using large CRT monitors allows for more desk space.

    - *A hands-free environment.* Softphones depend upon headsets. Most users love that! Headsets can be inexpensive wired units (about $30) or more expensive wireless units. Some wireless headsets are inexpensive, but my favorite one is a bit pricey (a little more than $300). Rather than using Bluetooth technology (often spotty performance), the Sennheiser Office Runner uses radio frequency technology that gives it up to a 400-foot crystal clear range!

    - *The ability to interface with the computer or device's contact list, like Outlook.* Using softphone apps means the softphones can interface with your contact list.

    - *Saving money.* Buying softphones is economical, costing less than handsets. The solution we prefer is Counterpath's Bria. Bria for Windows or Mac is about $50[26] with volume discounts available. Appropriate physical handsets—cheap

---

[26] Counterpath Corp., https://secure.counterpath.com/store/counterpath/.

ones—are at least double that; the ones my firm recommends cost less than $200.

- *Less Ethernet ports needed.* Using softphones eliminates the need for having two Ethernet ports at each desk (optimal configuration for desks with a computer and a handset)—more on that later.

• *Live Attendant or Automated Attendant?* Many churches still want a live person to answer phones rather than an automated attendant. VoIP PBXes give you multiple options, which are:

- Live attendant;

- Automated attendant greeting that gives options for service times and locations and a list of departments; it also encourages the caller to enter an extension if known, or to use a dial-by-name directory; or

- Live attendant backed up by an automated attendant when the live attendant isn't logged in or is unable to answer within a specified number of rings.

• *Hosted Off-Site or Locally On-Site?* One of the options especially helpful for churches located in regions that experience electrical outages throughout the year is the ability to have the PBX hosted in a datacenter. Many still prefer to have it hosted locally on-site at the church, but it's nice to have the option! When hosted in a datacenter, phone communications can still happen even in a power outage by using an internet connection somewhere or running a smartphone softphone app.

VoIP phones, whether handsets or softphones, log into the PBX server. Because they are IP phones, they can log into the PBX from anywhere they have an internet connection!

This feature serves mobile workforces in the church well. For instance, if pastors like to do their sermon prep from home, they can login their handset (if they have one at home) or softphone to the PBX and it's like they are just down the hall at the church office! You can simply call them on their regular extension.

Also, when someone changes offices, they can easily keep their extension—without calling a technician to program the system!

Using the smartphone softphone app to call someone shields the cell number in the caller ID, and instead sends the church's caller ID. This is helpful to protect church team members during off hours because it keeps everyone they call from learning their personal cell number.

One of our clients is a missions agency, and this aspect serves them *very* well. The agency's overseas office logs into the same hosted PBX as the home office, so the offices on both continents are simply extensions to each other. When team members travel overseas, they have the softphone app on their smartphone log into the PBX, and they are, again, simply an extension. They really like being able to get an outside line in the US, no matter their location. And there are no international dialing issues or long-distance rates!

Consider how helpful this feature would be for short-term mission trips. We recommend having a few extensions and softphone apps in reserve and ready to assign to short-term missions trip leaders. While on the trip, if leaders have WiFi access on their smartphones, they can securely call the church by simply dialing an extension—and can likewise receive calls!

Important VoIP Warnings

VoIP options may appeal to churches. They have their advantages, but they can also pose challenges. Several ways VoIP can cause problems include:

1. *Two Ethernet ports are required.* My firm is primarily known for data networks, and has had many clients who were previously sold a poorly set-up VoIP system from a phone company. The challenge is that most churches do not have two Ethernet ports at each desk (VoIP phones connect to the church network with an Ethernet cable just as computers do). To avoid the cost of pulling more cable drops so that each workstation has at least two ports available to it, many VoIP salespeople tell folks to plug the telephone handsets into the only available Ethernet port at their desks, and then plug the computers into the phones. Some VoIP phones can pass the data through, but they usually limit the data flow the computers want and need. As primarily data people, my firm is always displeased when that happens.

   This is another reason I like the softphone concept so much. It's almost like taking an algebraic equation and reversing what is on each side of the equal sign. Rather than plugging the computer into the phone, it's like plugging the phone into the computer. The phone requires very little bandwidth, so it doesn't suffer, and the computer gets all the bandwidth it needs. Win-win!

2. *VoIP PBXes can be vulnerable to hacking.* It is important to protect the PBX properly by putting it behind a capable firewall. Make certain you keep the PBX software and the server's OS current. Many of the patches released have security enhancements that are important to have in place.

SECTION THREE

Church IT Strategies

||||||||||||||||

Trying to predict the future is like trying to
drive down a country road at night with no
lights while looking out the back window.

Peter F. Drucker [27]

||||||||||||||||

---

[27] Peter Drucker. Origin unknown.

CHAPTER 12

IT Volunteers: Yes or No?

||||||||||||||||

We have different gifts, according to the
grace given to each of us. If your gift is ...

The Apostle Paul [28]

||||||||||||||||

For many reasons, churches thrive when their congregations are involved in the work of the church. We love—and need—our volunteers! They are crucial to churches.

What should you do with congregants who want to volunteer to help with your IT? There are ways IT volunteers can help and there are ways they can hurt. Let's address some common issues that cause problems for church teams when volunteers are involved. The goal here is to help church IT leaders effectively use volunteers and avoid common missteps in using those volunteers.

Also, someone who volunteers for a church IT team should understand the church's perspective and priorities so that their help is most effective.

---

[28]   Romans 12:6.

What Can Go Wrong?

When churches rely on IT volunteers, here are a few things that can go wrong:

1. Poor IT strategy. Churches often suffer from poor IT strategies because they allow people—volunteers and staff—to learn and develop their IT skills while serving the church in this vital area. Letting people learn and grow in the church IT Department sounds good, but the truth is that it is usually only good for the one learning and growing.

When these individuals are improving their knowledge and skills, they are doing so by trial and error because that's one of the ways people learn. The unfortunate result is a less-than-optimal IT strategy and solution, leading to unnecessary break downs and wasted time for the church staff. Lost productivity is costly.

2. Fragmented IT strategy. This is a compounding of the first point. When asked to evaluate or help with IT strategies, people bring the perspective of their experience. If that experience is different from those who came before, and it nearly always is, then any new strategy introduced will be based on the experience and perspective of the newest team member. That usually results in a fragmented IT strategy that doesn't mesh well with other strategies in place, affecting staff productivity. It will be magnified further if the perspectives invited to weigh in on the IT strategy have limited IT experience.

My firm saw this play out at a megachurch where a new congregant, who was a sales engineer for a large hardware manufacturer, introduced himself to one of the pastors after the service. When the pastor learned of the new congregant's employer, he invited him to evaluate the church's IT strategy. When the congregant did, he noted that the church experienced higher-than-normal reliability with zero downtime, but said its strategy wasn't *scalable*. (Scalability refers to the ability of a system to scale up to an extremely large configuration, like when a company goes global.) He recommended that the system be partially redone with scalability in mind.

The pastor agreed that scalability must be important since it is a church with global reach, so a plan and budget were created using equipment from the congregant's company. The budget was **huge**, and the size of the church ten years later is about the same as it was when the sales engineer—using a term few outside of IT fully understand—sold the church on the need to be scalable. It was terrible to see so much money wasted.

 3. Lack of availability. These poor and fragmented strategy issues mean increased support needs. And volunteers generally are not available when they are needed most: when church staff are at work. Volunteers are usually only available before or after work hours. More productivity is lost because problems can't be resolved until after hours. Although the church staff usually absorbs this for a while, the dynamic often creates conflict.

 4. Burnout. The problem comes full circle. Poor, fragmented IT strategies require more and more after-hours support from the volunteer, who eventually concludes that a choice must be made between supporting the IT strategies that he or she helped put into place or spending time with friends, family, and activities. If the volunteer pulls back or bows out, the church then must find another person to take over.

5. The cycle repeats, and things will likely get worse by further IT strategy fragmentation.

Church IT Complexity

The IT needs of churches are more sophisticated in their complexity than most realize! Here's why:

- *Sophisticated complexity*. Rather than a simple list of names and contact information, churches track many dimensions of congregants' lives, including contact information, family structures, life events, interests and spiritual gifts, volunteerism, background check data for certain volunteer roles (like children's workers, for example, to ensure no pedophiles are involved), contributions, attendance, and more. In addition, churches use many audio/visual solutions (hardware and software), and they need to run with the excellence and reliability of a broadcast studio.

- *Mission critical*. Church staffs are usually smaller in number than their for-profit counterparts and have less computer application training, but they still have deadlines that must be met every week. Dan Bishop with Houston CO-OP in Houston once said the church is more like a newspaper business with daily and weekly publication deadlines than almost any other business analogy. He is correct! Only a reliable system can relieve the level of stress these deadlines create for smaller teams—every week, on time, every time.

- *Budget sensitivity.* Churches with small teams, working with daily and weekly deadlines, also have limited budgets. Therefore, IT strategies need to tackle sophisticated complexity and mission critical reliability as efficiently as possible. Anything less will hinder the mission of the church.

The Right Place for IT Volunteers

A few professional IT vendors specialize in helping churches meet IT needs well. At the time of this writing, I know of four or five—two of whom have a national reach. At a minimum, they can help set the overall IT strategy in your church and identify roles in which volunteers can help.

Some possible volunteer IT roles that can be successful include:

- Help desk, if they're available during weekday work hours or on weekends to provide needed off-time for IT staff (see Chapter 14);

- Pulling cable;

- Moving equipment;

- Deploying/installing software (if given a step-by-step list to help achieve standardization among systems); and

- Some periodic maintenance routines, such as cleaning keyboards, mice, and monitors/displays.

Each of these is helpful and important, and inviting volunteers to help in these ways will be a blessing for staff members and volunteers alike.

Another way churches involve IT volunteers is to offer their communities free tech days. People in the community can bring their computers to the church to be updated, repaired, swept for viruses, and so on. What a terrific bridge-building event! In addition, it's a great way to let IT volunteers serve.

If your church hosts a free-tech day, my firm suggests that the person bringing a computer in for repair sign a release that covers such issues as:

- Liability (this is a free service);

- Inadvertent discovery of private information, such as ID numbers, credit card numbers, and so on;

- Inadvertent discovery of child porn or other illegal data with possible mandatory reporting rules that may apply.

CHAPTER 13

Training: The Most Neglected Spec

‖‖‖‖‖‖‖‖‖

Organized learning must become a lifelong process.

Peter F. Drucker [29]

‖‖‖‖‖‖‖‖‖

In Chapter 4, I described the best way to choose new solutions is by conducting a thorough analysis of needs and an objective search (see the section titled "A Better Way," beginning on page 43). When using this approach, the staff members will recognize that no solution is perfect and focus on the 80 percent to 85 percent of the needs the new solution will meet. Staff members will clean up their data, receive training, and begin enjoying the blessings of the transition.

Then normal change and growth begin to affect the staff. New people join the team through growth and attrition, but the new people were not part of the software search. They never had to go through the pain of cleaning up old data and were never trained. Two things begin to happen: (1) newcomers use the software incorrectly, degrading its effectiveness and the integrity of the data; and (2) as they struggle to understand how the software works, they look for alternative solutions that are simpler for only their or their department's needs. These dynam-

---

[29]   Peter Drucker, *Classic Drucker* (2006).

ics cause the entire staff's focus to shift from the 80 percent to 85 percent of the software that works well for the entire church to the portion that doesn't. Often, the church ends up concluding the current software doesn't work for them anymore, even though it mostly does. Lack of ongoing training is really at the heart of the problem.

Training is the Key

Whether it is ChMS or another technological tool used, your church should prioritize ongoing training for your teams. Few IT investments will yield better returns for a church.

The two areas of IT that most affect the entire staff are ChMS and productivity tools. Here are the strategies I recommend:

- *ChMS.* Require on-site training by the solution provider for all staff when implementing a new system. Require on-site training every year, too.

  This will:

  - Give your team members the ability to discuss their "pain points," so the trainer can either show ways to improve processes or communicate those pain points to the solution provider. Caution the staff not to fall into an unwillingness to change a process because "we've always done it that way."

  - Encourage your team to learn about new features the solution offers and emphasize how these features can help fulfill your ministry vision. It's essential that the solution continues to grow in its abilities to meet needs.

  - Train new team members on the solution.

- Help keep the team focused on the 80 to 85 percent of met expectations rather than the 15 to 20 percent of missed expectations.

There is a cost for this strategy, but it is well worth it.

- *Productivity Software.* The best resource I've seen for training on common software like Word, Excel, Creative Suite, and so on is subscribing to lynda.com. It is reasonably priced (most churches create one account that all can use, though only one can use it at a time), and a terrific resource for training on many applications and skill sets. Accountability is wise, so I recommend setting up a requirement (number of sessions or specific courses) that must be completed within a specific period of time for each team member.

A Great Example

One church impressed me more than any other in regard to its staff's productivity and efficiency. A staff member explained to me what the church does, and I now recommend their approach often:

- *Identify your specialists.* Look for team members who have a real passion and proficiency in each of your software solutions (word processing, spreadsheets, databases, and so on). Make these your specialists! Make certain you don't choose the same person for more than one or two solutions; spread the responsibility and acknowledgement around. Doing so also helps keep you from losing your entire knowledge base if that one person leaves.

- *Invest in your specialists.* When you identify your specialists, tell each one they have a budget for training to get even better with their respective solution. Add the requirement of outside training to their annual review to be certain they do it. This will also help them get training material ideas for training the rest of your team!

- *Schedule regular weekly, bi-weekly, or monthly training opportunities.* Here is how to do this well:

    - Require all non-credentialed administrative staff to attend the training.

    - Open the training sessions to credentialed administrative staff as well as non-administrative staff. Advertise among the team the topic of the next session so a credentialed or non-administrative team member can attend if it is something he or she wants to learn.

    - Rotate topics every session. For example, one week or month the topic might be how to do an email mail-merge, and another week or month the topic might be how to create a meaningful graphic dashboard using data from the ChMS database and accounting system.

This very powerful strategy costs little and accomplishes so much! The only way it works, though, is to have the full buy-in of the senior pastor or the person responsible for staff performance and development. Otherwise, some who need it most will always be too busy to attend, which will affect all others on staff, too. In addition, it requires a champion to coordinate the training and to see the plan through.

In addition to raising everyone's proficiency, other benefits of this strategy are that it will:

- Encourage people identified as specialists. Most people serving in these capacities are behind-the-scenes and rarely get public recognition for the quality of the work they do in fulfilling the vision of your church.

- Relieve IT staff from needing to train team members on how to use all of the solutions at your church. The specialist can become the primary person to help others learn how to use the solutions because the entire team begins to realize questions about a specific application are more appropriate for the specialist.

- Increase the ability of your entire team to fulfill the mission of your church.

A Security Training Tool

We recently ran across a security tool that trains your team on how to manage and handle email they receive.

Here's the challenge:

- We have many team members who feel they are too busy or can't be bothered with learning secure email practices.

- Many feel they know what they're doing already anyway.

- Many of those same people are the very ones who click on links in email that infect their computer or, worse, the network drive. Some get their identity stolen or, again even worse from an organizational perspective, transfer tens of thousands of dollars because someone duped them into believing the pastor or ministry leader wanted—or needed—them to.

Welcome to the rescue, KnowBe4.com[30]! This service lets you set up an account and design a campaign that sends your team emails that look real, but are actually like SPAM. Anyone who responds inappropriately (clicks a link, completes an embedded form, and so on) gets put into a kind of limbo, which he or she then can only escape by watching a short, well-done online video explaining what he or she did wrong.

KnowBe4 is "best of breed," and we recommend subscribing to the Platinum Tier. (**Note**: My firm was able to negotiate a great discount with KnowBe4 for churches and ministries. Any church or ministry that contacts the company (855.566.9234 or sales@knowbe4.com) and says MBS, Inc. referred it will receive a 55-percent discount.)

---

[30]   KnowBe4, Inc., http://knowbe4.com.

CHAPTER 14

How to Keep IT Staff in the Local Church

||||||||||||||||

The way a team plays as a whole determines
its success. You may have the greatest bunch
of individual stars in the world, but if they
don't play together, the club won't be worth
a dime.

Babe Ruth [31]

||||||||||||||||

The largest budget expense for most churches and ministries is the salaries and benefits paid to personnel. Sometimes another category, such as facilities, runs higher, but there's no getting around the fact that salaries and benefits consumes a large—if not the largest—portion of a budget.

We are called to be good stewards, or managers, of the resources we've been provided, so this category of expense is full of "good stewardship" opportunities!

One of the most challenging aspects of budget stewardship involves attracting and retaining quality staff members over time—especially

---

[31] Babe Ruth, http://BabeRuth.com/quotes/.

those in positions that focus on what would typically be considered *non*-ministry skillsets. IT is one such skillset.

Typical Approach

When hiring to fill open positions, we rightly look for individuals who are motivated by our missional focus. We want people who share our beliefs—who are sold out to our mission, and who are well-qualified to do the work for which they're being hired even as they grow in their own spiritual faith.

We also rightly look for individuals we can afford, again driven by the charge to be good stewards. Some churches consult salary guides, but honestly, not enough do. Among those churches that do consult salary guides, many probably only focus on those published specifically for Christian churches and ministries.

That can initially work. When someone pursues a new job with a church IT team, he or she mainly focuses on landing the position and those sources of salary information may be sufficient.

Over time, though, as this individual transitions from "new hire" status to a key member of the team, his or her skills and experience will grow. How can IT ensure it keeps this valuable worker relatively satisfied, as far as compensation and benefits are concerned, given the "going rate" for this person is likely much higher outside of ministry? This is a crucial question because the loss of that team member would be difficult on the entire staff and ministry.

My role gives me the chance to talk with a lot of IT people both in secular and ministry settings. Those who work for churches and ministries share these complaints most often:

- The work schedule (they have to work weekends when their friends are off and having fun).

- The high-stress demands by management to accomplish high reliability and to meet new needs— without a realistic amount of time or an appropriate expense budget for good equipment to do so.

- The low pay.

It's great to be motivated by the mission. But church and ministry leaders must understand the need to create effective supporting strategies that retain talented IT staff members—ones that sustain them in the midst of ministry demands, especially as friends and peers in related positions outside ministry often enjoy higher pay and better perks.

Work Environment

Pastors and those in ministry have many friends and colleagues in similar roles. That's true for most of us: we tend to develop relationships with others in similar roles and interests.

When that happens in non-ministry disciplines such as IT, it creates a sometimes-challenging tension because the different types of organizations (secular vs. ministry) approach IT so differently. Organizations that employ IT professionals vary widely in their approaches to work schedules, equipment budgets, professional development opportunities, and so on. Churches frankly don't tend to invest well in these areas for their teams. Here a few strategies to consider that can help:

- *Work Schedule*. Evaluate the church's culture and look for opportunities to encourage non-ministry discipline staff to take weekends off. A couple ways would be using a larger team that could rotate weekends and/or using volunteers that can support most needs during weekend services. These would be people who can reconnect devices to the network that have gone offline, add paper to label printers used for children's ministry check-ins, and so on. They don't need to have network expertise, admin network passwords, and the keys to the kingdom. They just need to help system users keep going in the rush of worship services (see also Chapter 12, under the section titled "The Right Place for IT Volunteers" beginning on page 99).

- *Equipment Budgets*. Churches and ministries look for ways to minimize overhead so they can focus as much budget money as possible on programs. That's appropriate. But church leaders would be wise to listen to IT team members when they give a cost estimate for something the ministry wants to accomplish. Rather than respond, "That's too high," leaders should consider the sophistication—and thus the higher costs—involved with technology needs. The technology for church projects and services is akin to configuring services for a convention center. Leadership, though, tends to assume the technological needs and tasks aren't challenging or won't cost too much, based on comparable, inexpensive set-ups for, say, a home. But this is not a home environment. The strategies, setups, and costs are very different.

- *Professional Development*. IT is a profession with constantly changing methodologies. Churches should fund professional development for IT staff members. Insist they attend one to two annual conferences. They need to do this if they are going to continue growing in their skills and get recharged. One of the better opportunities for this in the church IT field is the Church

IT Network.[32] This organization offers a high-quality annual conference every fall. And it is very inexpensive.

Compensation

Matthew Branaugh, editor of ChurchLawAndTax.com, once said, "One of the most effective tools available to churches is a salary survey." His organization runs ChurchSalary.com, which offers helpful information on a variety of church positions, though it doesn't yet include non-ministry-discipline positions like IT.

For non-ministry disciplines like IT, it is important to research beyond salary surveys specific to churches and ministries. To get the best picture of what these positions are worth, compare those with secular salary surveys to ensure whatever salary range you set is reasonable. The chart below is a comparison of three 2018 salary surveys—two that are church-specific and one that is secular—for two typical church IT positions.[33] [34] [35]

25% & 75% percentile	Robert Half	TCN's MinistryPay	LifeWay
Help Desk Tier 1	$32k - $45.5k	(IT Specialist/ Director only searchable option) $49.3k - $68.1k	(IT Specialist/ Director only searchable option) $35.3k - $49.3k
"Systems Engineer/ Network Administrator"	$85k - $121.5k		

Figure 4: Salary Survey Comparison

---

32   Church IT Network, http://ChurchITNetwork.com.
33   Robert Half, Robert Half 2018 Technology Survey 15 (2018).
34   The Church Network, http://ministrypay.com.
35   LifeWay, http://compstudy.lifeway.com.

Please note the following observations:

- MinistryPay's and LifeWay's terrific surveys, like many in the church and ministry field, don't differentiate between highly skilled non-ministry disciplines like IT and all other non-ministry disciplines. Their surveys would be helpful in setting a salary for the "Help Desk, Tier 1" role, but are not much help beyond that role.

- Robert Half's surveys always feel a little high to those of us in ministry, but they are more accurate of what the compensation of these two common church IT roles would be in the open marketplace and they get us closer to the right salary range. This information especially demonstrates why so many churches have a difficult time keeping highly skilled team members, such as a network administrator, from looking elsewhere for income and employment.

- Starting salaries vary from city to city and region to region. According to Robert Half, the reasons are cost of living, scarcity of top talent, and more. And the variances can be extreme! In some cities like San Francisco and New York, churches and ministries should add more than 40 percent to these numbers! And churches and ministries in places like Kalamazoo, Michigan, and Stockton, California should reduce those numbers by about 20 percent. It is important any survey figures are adjusted for geographic location accordingly.

This is not to say that a church needs to match the compensation possibilities available in the secular employment arena. Some will say that the ministry component (the IT person's buy-in to the mission of the organization) should override the IT person's drive for higher compensation. Mission should be a strong component—especially in an individual's early years of church employment.

But if the IT person has proven invaluable to the organization, then the disparity between the church and secular salary guides must be balanced—that is, if the organization wants to keep the individual on staff long-term.

Remember, the cost of replacing a key team member is higher than the cost of keeping one by increasing his or her salary and/or bene-fits. Good stewardship can include reasonably increasing those costs to keep a quality IT team member.

CHAPTER 15

IT Staff: Insource or Outsource?

||||||||||||||||

Only do what only you can do.

Andy Stanley [36]

||||||||||||||||

At one time, there might have been one computer in a church, most likely in the accounting office. The use of computers has grown dramatically since those early days of church computing. Now every staff member has at least one computer—or access to at least one. Computers are terrific tools that can powerfully help every team member become more productive and efficient!

With the expansion of computer use, each church will likely reach the point of realizing regular computer help is needed. That is when the church looks at bringing in a specialist.

But should the church "insource" by hiring the specialist as a full-time staff member? Or should the church "outsource" by hiring a firm or someone as an independent contractor? Understanding the four different IT roles in churches and how they differ (see Chapter 1) is helpful when deciding whether to insource or outsource.

---

[36]   Andy Stanley, *Next Generation Leader: Five Essentials for those who will shape the Future* (2006).

Most of the time outsourcing some of the support responsibility *is* a better strategy!

What IT Roles Are In Play?

In multisite megachurches, all four IT roles are at a level that it makes sense to hire in-house specialists. What about small- to large-sized churches (under 2,000 in average weekly worship attendance)? The answer changes to *maybe* it makes sense to hire in-house. The decision revolves around what IT disciplines are the most heavily used. Those disciplines are (see Chapter 1 for more details):

- Web and graphic design;
- Audio/video;
- Social media; and
- Data infrastructure.

In small- to large-sized churches, one person usually fills all of those needs, even though it is unlikely the person has the appropriate depth in all four disciplines. That's when it makes great sense to outsource some of the responsibility. Doing so allows the church to benefit from large strategies,[37] even though the church cannot afford to hire someone full- time who possesses the levels of expertise needed to bring those large strategies in.

Acknowledging My Bias

I need to pause and acknowledge my bias here. I sensed the Lord's call to help Christian churches and ministries in this area, and established a company (MBS, Inc.) that is an outsource resource. I believe my company helps fill the data infrastructure side of outsourcing well

---

[37] By large strategies, I mean those IT strategies developed through working with many organizations to improve system reliability, reduce overall costs, and minimize the distractions problematic systems force on staff. The more systems one has done and had to support over time, the larger the strategy becomes to deliver reliability.

(and by God's grace, our clients seem to agree). So, I am a believer in the outsourcing model.

I have had the privilege of serving and consulting countless churches and ministries nationwide for more than three decades. I have seen patterns of how churches approach this issue. Some work well. Some do not. Given that perspective, I offer a few thoughts here that may help.

Strategies that Increase IT Staff Size

My firm consulted with a large church that wanted to know if its IT Department was what it should be. They wanted us to evaluate their department efficiency, size, and quality. We conducted what we call an IT Audit to accomplish that. What we discovered was surprising:

- The entire ministry staff was about 100 people. Sixteen of them were in the IT Department! The IT staff cost the organization more than $500,000 annually!

- The ministry had developed a few IT philosophies, or strategies, that drove the department to grow to such a large size:

  - Rather than buy enterprise-class hardware of an appropriate quality, the department bought inexpensive parts and built the computers and servers to save money. The true cost to maintain that hardware, though, included a number of full-time salaries—year after year.

  - The church's corporate culture included inviting the entire team to dream about what IT tools they'd like that would help them in their ministry. More than half of the IT Department consisted of programmers to create the apps the rest of the staff requested. The programmers also had to maintain them. Surprisingly, no one had checked to determine which were still in use!

There are strategies that can reduce the need for IT staff, and can save churches a lot of money. Here are a few:

- Buy enterprise-class hardware, and get at least a three-year warranty from the manufacturer with any of that hardware. Though letting desktop and notebook warranties expire after three years makes sense, servers—which are computers the entire ministry must be able to depend on 24/7/365—should always be kept under warranty. Dell, for example, will extend the warranty on a server to a total of seven years! After that, a server should be retired or put in a non-critical role.

- Eliminate custom apps wherever possible. They are costly to create and to maintain.

- Outsource all but what you can't. Though we encourage you to keep help-desk functionality in-house, other tasks, including engineering, programming, and pulling cable, and so on, are good candidates for outsourcing.

When to Outsource

Though it depends on how much small- to large-sized churches use graphics in their communications or A/V in their worship services, it seems the people most often sought for insourcing have great strengths in these disciplines. This most likely happens because—more often than not—communications and worship services are the first area with felt-needs for IT expertise. While these people may use vendors or church members to augment their skills in graphic artistry, for some reason they are often reluctant to do so in the data structure side of IT.

The assumption is typically that the IT needs for data structure are simple: give everyone full access to whatever they want and let the staff mostly manage themselves! These systems are mostly approached with what is now called a BYOD (Bring Your Own Device) strategy.

That is okay, unless there are also servers, public WiFi, and data responsibilities to manage; if so, it makes sense to outsource. While a church may be able to get by with outsourcing as needed for web and graphic design, audio/visual, and social media needs, a much more formal approach is necessary for outsourcing data infrastructure needs.

Who Can You Trust?

In Chapter 12, I described the best approach to using volunteers in IT, which is to address the three facets of church IT needs: sophistication and complexity, mission critical dependence, and budget sensitivity (see "Church IT Complexity" beginning on page 98). With those facets in mind, a good outsource resource in the data infrastructure discipline should meet the following minimal criteria to serve a church well:

• *Data Infrastructure Expertise*. Because a church's IT needs are sophisticated and complex, a good IT outsource resource should have deep experience in strategizing, designing, and supporting local area networks and cloud-hosted solutions for many organizations of a size similar to your church and larger. This large perspective requires strategies that minimize downtime and support needs. If your team needs to use your church's systems without distraction, this is important.

- *Church IT Expertise.* Because a church's IT needs are mission critical and budget sensitive, a good outsource resource should have the experience of working with many churches and ministries. Otherwise, it is likely the firm will not understand the mission critical nature of how church teams rely on their systems to fulfill their calling, while also meeting the constant flow of weekly deadlines. The natural inclination will be to utilize costly over-spec'd systems sold by the resource (which wastes funds) or consumer-class systems that cannot meet the reliability needs of the staff. Neither is a good use of funds, and those with church IT expertise know that.

- *Church Software Expertise.* Just like hospitals use software unique to their needs, as do accounting, legal, and engineering firms, churches use unique software to meet their needs. Whether it's your ChMS database, a nonprofit accounting package, presentation software, or event scheduling and registration software, the outsource resource needs to know how those systems work and what they require. Some have very specific and unique requirements, and delivering reliability means knowing how to configure the systems so the underlying infrastructure is supportive to them.

Screening IT Vendors

Most churches around the US will look for *local* IT vendors to save the funds that would have been spent on travel with an out-of-the-area vendor. In the previous section I gave you four things to look for in a vendor, but what additional factors should one look for? Here are a few more thoughts that may help:

- Ask for references of organizations similar to yours (number of servers, WiFi access points, desktops, and notebooks/tablets).

- Call a few of the references and ask how long they've been using the vendor.

- A great question to ask is, "If you had to look for a new vendor, what would you do differently?"

- Check any customer satisfaction resources that might be available. One you might check with is the Better Business Bureau where the vendor is based.

One of the key considerations when looking for an IT vendor is to look for one with multiple staff. My firm recently spoke with a church that used an IT vendor that was a one-person shop. The church felt he served well, but he did not document the church's system. When he died, it was up to the church, or the church's next IT vendor, to figure out how the system was configured. That took time and cost money, and until it was completed the church's team suffered from more costly support, due to the extra time needed for discovering each support need.

I previously mentioned that my firm is an outsource resource. It's important to note that there are a few other firms who also focus on serving churches, regionally and/or nationally, well. Here is a list of the four, in alphabetical order (my firm included, of course!):

- ACTS Group (http://actsgroup.net)
- BEMA (http://bemaservices.com)
- MBS, Inc. (http://mbsinc.com)
- Enable Resource Group (formerly Solerant) (https://enableresourcegroup.com)

Remember that the homework your church does upfront with IT out-sourcing can make a crucial difference with your church's short- and long-term IT success. Research the data infrastructure, hardware, and software expertise the vendor possesses with churches. Talk with other clients (ideally other churches and ministries) to find out the vendor's strengths and weaknesses. And make sure the vendor employs multiple people to ensure continuity and consistency.

CHAPTER 16

Who Owns Your Public DNS Record?

||||||||||||||

Dovorey no provorey. That means trust,
but verify.

Ronald Reagan [38]

||||||||||||||

DNS stands for Domain Name System, and it is the worldwide method to help people find things on the internet. For instance, opening a browser and typing in the address field "mbsinc.com" will take you to my firm's website.

Figure 5: DNS Servers: A Worldwide Network

---

[38]   President Ronald Reagan, Remarks at a Senate Campaign Rally for Christopher S. Bond in Springfield, Missouri, (Oct. 23, 1986).

DNS is how the internet knows where our website is. It stores the server IP address for each website and more.

DNS runs on innumerable servers around the world, so that regardless of where your website is hosted, someone anywhere in the world can connect to it.

Your church's public DNS record is the record the internet uses to point others to your websites, your email server, and potentially much more. So, who owns your public DNS record and why does it matter?

Why is DNS Record Ownership Important?

One way to think of DNS is to think of your street address or home phone number. Both are important in how people in your community reach you, and an interruption would mean that people would not easily find you. In today's culture, if an attempt to find you takes too long or fails, an individual will likely lose interest and move on.

That is exactly what happens when someone tries to get to your website or send you an email. With even a minimal delay, let alone a problem, people will simply move on.

Having control of your public DNS record means you can fix a problem if one occurs, and you can keep one from developing in the event of an employee or member disagreement or a controversy in the church.

Public DNS Record Access

Technology is constantly changing. When you change or add IT services (like email or instant messaging), change internet service providers, change server configurations, and so on, doing so often requires making a change to your public DNS record. More likely than not, there will come a time when someone working with your website or email system will want to make a change to your public DNS record. We often encounter this as we begin working with new clients. Many times, no one at the church knows how to access and modify the DNS record. The most common reasons why are:

- A volunteer or staff member created the church's first website or email server, and set up a DNS record accordingly. At the time, it was done under this person's name with his or her credentials (user ID and password), and he or she never thought to properly document it or transfer it into the church's name.

- When the church set up its first website or email server, the web host set up the DNS for it.

Both situations need to be addressed, and here is why:

- In the case of DNS record ownership by a volunteer or staff member, what happens when the relationship with that person and your church ends? For various reasons, volunteers sometimes change churches, as do team members. In either case, if DNS ownership moves with them, making future changes will be more difficult than it should be. It could be even more difficult if the person has died, and the record ownership is in probate or with heirs who are not friendly to your church.

- All businesses—churches included—need the freedom to change vendors at any time and for any reason. If a web host holds ownership to the church's DNS record, making a change in that relationship can be problematic. An employee of the web host could try to use the DNS record as a bargaining chip to keep your church's business there.

What Is The Best Approach?

My firm's new clients often ask us if we want to take on their DNS record ownership. Our answer is always no. We need access to it to do our work, but the church should maintain ownership of its DNS record.

We usually recommend the church move its DNS record to DNS Made Easy.[39] Its annual fee is reasonable, and this keeps the DNS record in a neutral environment. The church can grant access to whomever it wants as needed, or revoke that access as needed.

If you don't know who owns your church's DNS record, this should be a high priority. Find out where it is, who has access to it, and take ownership of it.

---

[39] DNS Made Easy, http://dnsmadeeasy.com.

CHAPTER 17

Disaster Recovery and Business Continuity

||||||||||||||||

Be prepared!

Boy Scout Motto [40]

||||||||||||||||

Disasters of all types happen, and they can happen at any time. That's why there's a robust news reporting industry—every day there are new

disasters to talk about! Some are natural, some are manmade, but they all disrupt lives.

September 11, 2001, changed many things in the US. More lives were lost in the three attacks that day than were lost in the Pearl Harbor attack on December 7, 1941.[41] No one knows how many businesses were also killed that day, but it's safe to say that the number was large because the data necessary to sustain their

Figure 6: First Baptist Church in Gulfport, Miss., after Hurricane Katrina hit

---

40   Boy Scouts of America, http://usscouts.org/advance/boyscout/bsoathlaw.asp.
41   National Commission on Terrorist Attacks Upon the United States, The 9/11 Commission Report Executive Summary 2, (July 22, 2004).

operations (accounts receivable, accounts payable, various documents and spreadsheets, databases, and so on) was not properly backed up.

The same is true of major *natural* disasters, such as hurricanes, tsunamis, tornadoes, earthquakes, and fires. This is a picture of a church that was severely impacted by Hurricane Katrina.[42] Many appropriately consider disaster recovery to be one of IT's highest priorities.

Backup Strategies

The goal of any good backup strategy is to protect data from threats that could destroy it. There are many backup strategies. The best are automatic, comprehensive, tested, and include an off-site storage component. Here are details on all of those:

- *Automatic.* Manually initiated backups are guaranteed to fail. Backups aren't needed very often, and any computer user can easily fall into the *I don't have time today* syndrome, which then develops into a backup system that is never run. Backups should run regularly, automatically, and unattended. There are software solutions that can automate backups. My favorite is Veeam.[43]

- *Comprehensive.* I am not a fan of partial backups, sometimes referred to as incremental backups. The problem is that when restoring data, time is usually tight. The longer it takes to find all the needed files and restore them, the more stressful the situation becomes. A comprehensive backup avoids that stress.

---

[42] First Baptist Church in Gulfport, Miss. (2005). Photo by Greg Warner. Used with permission.
[43] Veeam Software, http://veeam.com.

- *Tested.* There's nothing worse than running your first backup test while trying to recover from a disaster, and *then* learning that the backups weren't doing what you hoped. I learned this the hard way when my team and I were helping a client replace the Network Operating System (NOS) of a server. Our first step was to run a comprehensive backup and have the backup software confirm that the backup was good by comparing file names, dates, and sizes. Once that was done, we deleted the server's partitions (effectively erasing any possible data on the hard drives), then we installed the new NOS, installed the backup software, and then restored the backup we had just created. We were shocked to learn that the backup, though it passed the compare test, was worthless! All of the characters in the files were null characters (null characters look like this: ☐)! Using some tech tools, we restored most of the data, but it made for a long and embarrassing night.

- *Include an off-site component.* A copy of a recent backup needs to be taken off-site in case there's a disaster large enough to take out the server room. The September 11 attacks on the Twin Towers and the flooding from Hurricane Katrina damaged or destroyed many on-site server rooms. The off-site backup must be comprehensive. It cannot be an incremental backup. Some prefer online backup solutions, such as Carbonite or CrashPlan, to accomplish this. More about that shortly.

Backups come in many flavors and strategies. Differences between backups include incremental *vs.* comprehensive, system level *vs.* file-level, server-only *vs.* server plus computers *vs.* computers-only, and more. The server component is further complicated if your servers are virtual machines running on a host using a hypervisor like VMware or HyperV.

What I Recommend and Why

Networks and computers store data. Some data is mission-critical, but not all of it. Even still, a loss of any and all data would take a lot of time to re-create and would slow down productivity while doing so.

I recommend backing up the entire system. The objection sometimes voiced is that doing so would require a lot of capacity. Appropriate capacity is reasonably inexpensive, and it needs to be seen in a similar light as an insurance policy.

For networks with servers and computers, I recommend the following:

- Configure all computers so they save their data to the server by default. It will save time and money not having to back up each computer on the network.

- Back up servers that store data every night. Do not run incremental backups—only run full backups. If the servers are virtual, use a backup solution, such as Veeam, that backs up the servers so they can be quickly restored in their entirety if necessary.

- Back up to tape drives. A good strategy is to have at least 20 tapes (four weeks' worth), and to rotate them daily. Label them as Week 1 – Monday, Week 1 – Tuesday, and so on through Friday; Week 2 – Monday, Week 2 – Tuesday, and so on through Friday; and Week 3 and Week 4 similarly. This will be helpful if someone discovers that an important file is corrupt, and the last time they had a good copy was three weeks ago, for example. Larger churches might choose to back up to an enterprise-class Network Attached Storage (NAS) or Storage Area Network (SAN) device. Those who don't have those devices should avoid backing up to external portable hard drives. External portable hard drives have many moving parts and are susceptible to breakage, which would render the backup on that device unusable without an expensive restoration process that may take more than a week and *may* work. Backing up to tape is still Corporate America's preference.

- Take one tape off-site each week, rotating it with the tape from the previous week. If, like most churches, your biggest data processing day of the week is Monday or Tuesday, the backup made the night of your biggest data processing day is the one that should be rotated off-site each week. That way you can always get back to within a week of your data if a large catastrophe impacts your church.

- If you're a large church and backing up to an enterprise-class NAS or SAN, you will want to setup a second NAS or SAN off site with data replication (an automated process in which one of these devices automatically replicates its data over a cable or internet connection) to accomplish the geographic separation component of your backup strategy. To save money, some churches 'partner' with another church in which they replicate to each other's sites. For instance, Church A might put a NAS or SAN in Church B's server room, and vice versa.

- Test your backups on at least a monthly basis. Keep an accountability spreadsheet to identify the backup data that was tested, the date it was tested, and what portion of the data structure was tested. The spreadsheet will help ensure that different sections of the data are tested and that, in fact, the testing happens.

What about Online Backups?

Online backup solutions are good for consumers' computers but not necessarily good for servers. The amount of data that would need to be transmitted over the internet to restore a server is usually so large that it could take weeks to download it all from an online service. Online services offer to send a copy on a hard drive if needed quickly, but the organizations I know that tried this approach were not pleased with the results.

Online backups are usually good for consumers who want to back up their data files, such as photos. Some clients of ours still use an online backup service to automate the off-site requirement and only use them to restore single files; they also have an on-site backup in case of a more severe disaster.

Setting an Appropriate Backup Budget

All technology costs something and thus requires a budget. Many in IT assume all data needs to be quickly restorable at all times. That strategy, however, may be too costly and beyond the reach of most churches.

The best way to set the backup strategy and budget is to ask church leadership to prioritize various categories of data and assign a maximum timeframe within which data must be restored following a disaster. In addition to helping set an appropriate backup system budget, this will help leadership think in terms of business continuity. (Business Continuity Plans detail how to continue operations in and following a major disaster.)

Typical categories of data include audio and video files, databases, email, and productivity documents like word processing files, spreadsheets, and so on. You may even want to break those categories down further to help leadership with this task. For instance, word processing files might include letters, bulletins, policies and procedures, and so on.

Often, leadership will assign the highest priority to communication systems and databases—email, financial databases, and non-financial databases. An example would be that email, telephones, and ChMS databases need to be restored within two hours, and everything else within three days.

After leadership assigns time frames for data restoration, design a backup strategy to meet the requirements and present it for approval. If leaders think the budget is too high, ask them to adjust some of the time frames they assigned to the data categories so you can redesign the strategy accordingly.

Business continuity is leadership's responsibility and disaster recovery is IT's responsibility. The only way a backup strategy budget can be appropriately set is with leadership's guidance.

How I Back Up Data

My firm hosts servers for many Christian churches and ministries in a high-end datacenter. We use Veeam to back up those servers, which gives us the ability to restore individual files or complete servers quickly. Our company's servers are also in our datacenter, so our data is protected.

The way we host file servers is unique, and is a helpful illustration for this chapter. We put all of our clients' data files in a file server that is all theirs—not shared with any other clients. We use a solution called Owncloud to provide access to data files. It works very much like Dropbox, but it has better security, and the data is private (though sharable). The data synchronizes to team members' hard drives (just like Dropbox), so it is almost as if they have second copies through that method.

I use a MacBook Pro that has a very large hard drive. On my Mac, I have Owncloud replicate our firm's entire data structure (not our clients' data, just ours). Granted, that takes Owncloud a little longer to synchronize, but there is a terrific benefit. The macOS includes a great app called Time Machine, which backs up my entire hard drive to an external drive whenever I am working at my desk. I use an external backup drive that is big enough to maintain more than a year's worth of Time Machine backups. In addition to the other protections my firm has in place, I can also quickly access all of our data with file versioning going back more than a year to find that last uncorrupted version of a file when needed!

Redundancy of backup layers is helpful. When I can find a file that was discovered to be corrupt or missing, team members see me as heroic! At times like that, the little extra spent to have that extra layer of protection is never thought of as an over expenditure.

CHAPTER 18

The Twelve Months of IT

||||||||||||||

A small behavioral change can also lead to
embracing a wider checklist of healthier
choices.

Chuck Norris [44]

||||||||||||||

If disaster recovery is one of IT's greatest responsibilities, how does one stay on top of it? The answer for me is checklists. *Checklists* means I don't have to try to remember to do certain things.

Setting up checklists can help eliminate the need to remember lists of tasks. Some might dismiss the need for checklists, but they are the key to avoiding letting things slip through the cracks. My favorite tool for checklists is Microsoft Outlook, where I can create recurring tasks that show up monthly, quarterly, annually, and so on.

Monthly Task Checklists

As I consider monthly tasks for IT, I almost find myself singing *The Twelve Days of Christmas*! Here is a list for consideration.

---

[44] Chuck Norris, Chuck Norris Simplifies Healthy Living, WND (June 24, 2016), https://www.wnd.com/2016/06/chuck-norris-simplifies-healthy-living/.

January

❑ Test backup quality by restoring a folder in the data structure that is different from any recent tests.

❑ January is the month of new beginnings, so seek out those on the team who have been there less than a year and ask them if there's anything their system could do to better serve them in their ministry. Then pray for their success in your organization's ministry.

February

❑ Test backup quality by restoring a folder in the data structure that is different from any recent tests.

❑ February is the month of love, so schedule a task that is an expression of love toward your user base. One idea: schedule a team of volunteers to come in on a midweek evening to clean users' mice, keyboards, and monitor/display screens. Encourage the volunteers to pray for the person who uses the workstation as they clean it, possibly for protection from the enemy—for them and their family—and for their effectiveness in ministry.

March

❑ Test backup quality by restoring a folder in the data structure that is different from any recent tests.

❑ March is the month of St. Patrick's Day, whose associated color is green. Do something good environmentally, like remove debris and organize the server room, and clean the fans and insides of the servers from dust.

❑ Pray for God's protection of the servers, switches, related equipment, and the data they contain.

April

❏ Test backup quality by restoring a folder in the data structure that is different from any recent tests.

❏ April starts with April Fools' Day, so check your system for peripheral equipment foolishly added by well-meaning team members (routers and switches, printers, and so on). Schedule follow-up time to help the users who introduced those devices. Help them understand the need to involve IT to determine their needs and coordinate ways to meet them. End the time with prayer for them, their family's protection from the enemy, and for their effectiveness in ministry.

May

❏ Test backup quality by restoring a folder in the data structure that is different from any recent tests.

❏ May is the month we observe Memorial Day in the US. Evaluate the church's hardware and software and identify which ones need their end of service scheduled. Begin planning for their replacements—or their elimination if no longer needed.

June

❏ Test backup quality by restoring a folder in the data structure that is different from any recent tests.

❏ June is the first month of summer in the US. Help those who will be going on vacation by making certain essential data others may need to access during their absence is located on a part of the church's network that does not require private passwords. Ask them if they'd like you to review how to set email and voicemail out-of-office greetings, and then how to turn them off again. Encourage them to completely unplug digitally while away, and pray for their safety and refreshment while on vacation.

July

❑ Test backup quality by restoring a folder in the data structure that is different from any recent tests.

❑ July is the month the US celebrates its independence, which is a good reminder that team members often act independently with regard to data and solutions. Encourage your team to share with you ways they have done so (without reprisals, of course), so you can help them understand ways the system is already designed to meet their needs in ways they may not have known, or help you understand ways the system needs to meet their needs better. End by praying for them and their family's protection from the enemy and for their effectiveness in ministry.

August

❑ Test backup quality by restoring a folder in the data structure that is different from any recent tests.

❑ This is the month when many return from vacation. This is a good time to review and upgrade systems so they're ready for the team's use as the fall, winter, and spring programs kick in. It's also a good time to pray for your organization's success in ministry.

September

❑ Test backup quality by restoring a folder in the data structure that is different from any recent tests.

❏ September begins in the US with Labor Day. This is a good time to schedule training and offer support appointments for team members.

October

❏ Test backup quality by restoring a folder in the data structure that is different from any recent tests.

❏ October is the month of Halloween, which is a good reminder that the enemy wants to do anything he can to disrupt your organization's ministry impact. In addition to checking system protection points (anti-malware, anti-SPAM, and firewall solutions), this is a good time to remind the team of the enemy's intent to do the ministry harm and enlist their prayer for the protection of the church's systems and data.

November

❏ Test backup quality by restoring a folder in the data structure that is different from any recent tests.

❏ November is the month of Thanksgiving in the US. This is a good time to thank our supervisors for the opportunity to serve on the team. It's also a good time to express gratitude to our biggest support challenges for their efforts and impact on the ministry.

December

❏ Test backup quality by restoring a folder in the data structure that is different from any recent tests.

❏ In December we remember God's greatest gift to us: forgiveness through Jesus Christ. This is a great time to think through each member of the team and pray for them—for them and their family's protection from the enemy and for their effectiveness in ministry—and then send them an email or text letting them know you prayed for them and are excited about the ways they contribute to the organization's ministry.

You will likely have some additional items to add to your monthly checklists. Make certain to keep the list from being only tactical; keep spiritual components in it. You'll find they help you!

- Your team members will see you as a ministry partner rather than an adversary; and

- Doing so will help you avoid ministry burnout.

"No institution can possibly survive if it needs geniuses or supermen to manage it. It must be organized in such a way as to be able to get along under a leadership composed of average human beings," said Peter F. Drucker.[45]

---

45   Peter F. Drucker, https://www.brainyquote.com/quotes/peter_drucker_130664.

CHAPTER 19

The Security Sweet Spot

‖‖‖‖‖‖‖‖‖‖‖‖

Find the "sweet spot" between absolute
transparency and non-transparency—it's
called appropriate transparency—where
trust is maximized with minimal disruption
or risk to the ministry.

Dan Busby [46]

‖‖‖‖‖‖‖‖‖‖‖‖

Chapter 2 explained the importance of team members being thought of as customers of the church's IT Department. The chapter also described some of the ramifications of that approach to managing technology in churches. One topic in that chapter was giving *local admin* status to all team members (see "Here Are a Couple of Practical Examples," beginning on page 27), which some argue is a weakening of the church's system security. On page 28, I mention two ways to overcome those security concerns.

Additional customer satisfaction issues for team members include our firm's approach to password strategies, off-site file access, and WiFi access. How one approaches security affects each of these.

---

[46]   Dan Busby, *Trust* (2015).

Security Is Important!

Strong system security is critical. Much of the data we have in churches is sensitive: the most common are counseling notes, board minutes, HR documentation, contributions information, and database records. Churches need to do their due diligence to protect all of it.

Many people today question anything less than a full-access approach to church data. However, some of the data that churches have can harm people or the church if let into the wild.

Consider these scenarios:

- In some states, like California, where I live, there is a state constitutional right to privacy. If I were a terminated church employee and my termination details or contact information was not properly safeguarded by the church, and I felt somehow harmed by that lack of protection, I could sue for a violation of my right to privacy.

- A church board is working through a sticky issue, such as the possible church discipline of a member as detailed in Matthew 18, and has referenced its discussion in its minutes. That is sensitive information that could hurt the individual and the church if it were not adequately protected.

- A church's vendor realized the value of the church's database and exported a copy of it. The vendor then began renting it as a list in the community. Consider the contents of that database and the possible damage it could do! The database included contact information, children's names, tithing records, life events, Social Security Numbers of employees, and more. This is a true story!

A church's data must be protected with firewalls and passwords.

The Right to Disappear from Your System

In May of 2018 the European Union's General Data Protection Regulation, or GDPR, went into effect. Many wondered about how it would impact US churches and ministries. The quick answer is that the EU doesn't have any jurisdiction in the US, so it doesn't have any legal impact on churches or ministries—unless that church or ministry has a physical presence in an EU country.

But understanding why the GDPR was enacted may provide a more important answer. GDPR addresses whether someone can ask to be removed from a database and have a reasonable assurance they will be. People, for a variety of reasons, sometimes want to be forgotten or removed from a list. You could call this the "Golden Rule of Database Management."

Unless there is a legal reason why it would be unwise to remove someone from your database, why not simply accommodate this individual? Treating others like we'd like to be treated is always a win-win, and a great way to honor Christ in our data management.

With that in mind, note that you should consult with your church's legal counsel if you receive a request from someone who wants to be removed from your church's database. Some reasons why your church may not be able to remove someone include:

- This person made contributions that were posted to your system.
- This person was an employee and has human resource and payroll records your church needs to keep.
- This person was a vendor who received payments from your church.

- This person was a volunteer who served in a position that required a background check.

Before you make a decision regarding a person's request to be removed, talk with your church's attorney to make certain the removal will not create unintended future liability for your church.

Password Strategies

Many churches have annual audits performed by CPA firms, often to satisfy the terms of building loans or to help demonstrate integrity in their finances to a watching world. Both are good reasons, and CPA audits are very helpful in many ways.

The Sarbanes-Oxley Act of 2002 was enacted in response to accounting scandals in some very large companies. One of its many effects is that CPA auditors now ask about many IT issues. This is part of their due diligence to see if things are being done correctly. Most of those auditors, however, do not have professional IT training or experience, and simply work through a series of questions and record responses.

Through this process CPAs have heightened everyone's sense of appropriate IT security. Some things they brought attention to are very good, such as locked server rooms. However, on password strategies, they may have hurt us by requiring we force password changes every ninety days. The practice of changing passwords so often in churches actually *lowers* security! Church team members are like most computer users. When they change their passwords they often write them on Post-It® notes, or tape them to their monitors and displays, or place them under keyboards or a desk drawer.

In a March 2, 2016, post on the US Federal Trade Commission's website, policies requiring regular password changes proved "less beneficial than previously thought, and sometimes even counterproductive."[47] They go on in that post to reference two university studies that caused them to draw the conclusion that "frequent mandatory [password] expiration inconveniences and annoys users without as much security benefit as previously thought, and may even cause some users to behave less securely."

I have been saying that for years!

What my firm recommends is the following password policy:

- Passwords must be a minimum of seven characters and include uppercase and lowercase alpha characters, numbers, and common punctuation. This is a great minimum in that it accommodates most Bible references! Perhaps your favorite verse is John 11:35. Consider a password like jOhN11.35—when a password is constructed this way, some refer to it as "hardened." As long as the verse is not super common, like John 3:16, it would take a *very* long time to break.

- Passwords must never be shared with others, and they should never expire. They will be replaced if a breach occurs.

- Passwords can only be set by the IT Department and are maintained in an encrypted file for use when supporting system users.

This policy makes for easy-to-remember passwords since it accommodates verse references. This helps to eliminate the Post-It® note

---

[47] Lorrie Cranor, Time to Rethink Mandatory Password Changes, Federal Trade Commission (March 2, 2016), http://ftc.gov/news-events/blogs/techftc/2016/03/time-re-think-mandatory-password-changes. See also Surprising New Password Guidelines from NIST, Password Ping, http://passwordping.com/surprising-new-password-guidelines-nist/.

issue. If people tell IT they need a new password because they shared it with someone, IT can give them a new one and update their encrypted documentation. If someone does that often, the situation should be referred to leadership for possible action.

Multi-Factor Authentication

Multi-Factor Authentication, or MFA, as it is sometimes known, engages two or more kinds of authentication factors consisting of:

1. *Knowledge*: something only the user *knows* (like a password, passphrase, or security question);
2. *Possession*: something only the user *has* (an identity card or USB key); and
3. *Inherence*: something only the user *is* (biometrics like a fingerprint, finger veins, retina, or facial recognition).

Another form of MFA is Two-Factor Authentication (sometimes called 2FA). As the term suggests, it uses two of the factors mentioned above.

These systems can be set up in various ways or combinations. One common method is to use a 2FA process in which one of the authenticating factors is sent to another device and entered—such as a code sent to a smartphone.

This may be a good way to increase system security, and churches are wise to consider it because it can prevent some attacks. But most church and ministry system users don't like the additional steps. There are also technological reasons why the increased security may be more of a *perceived* security improvement than an *actual* improvement. For instance, many "account recovery" processes bypass mobile phone 2FA, providing a potential workaround for a hacker.[48] That said, MFA is worth considering.

Firewalls

A firewall is a solution that keeps unwanted outsiders from accessing your computer systems. We need to guard against internet bots and people—the two major threats from the outside. Here's more details on both:

- Internet bots are little apps that roam the internet looking for exploitable ports into networks and computers. They are incessant, and their technology is constantly morphing into new threats. For that reason, it is essential that firewalls receive constant updates to help them identify new technology threats. Many firewall companies offer an annual subscription to meet this need.

- People who want to gain access into networks and computers include former employees, family members, and others in the community. Some have no malicious intent, but some do. The fact that some have bad intentions is why it is essential to have a policy of never sharing passwords.

Firewalls, aided by good password strategies, help protect churches from these threats.

There are software firewalls and hardware firewalls. Either can be good, depending on their spec. My firm's favorite spec is the Dell SonicWALL firewall series. SonicWALLs provide the features that most

---

48 See the "Disadvantages" section at https://en.wikipedia.org/wiki/Multi-factor_authentication.

churches need at a reasonable cost while not overcharging them for many features they will likely never use.

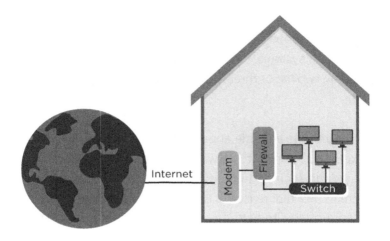

Figure 7: Diagram of a Firewall's position

One of SonicWALL's features that my firm likes is that it can also filter internet content; this prevents people using the church's WiFi from getting to websites the church considers inappropriate.

A good firewall and a good password policy help protect certain sensitive data from those outside the church who shouldn't have access to it. Firewalls and password policies can enforce access rules that augment the network security systems in place. In Figure 7, note that the internet connection comes in to a modem (sometimes called a router). Rather than plugging computers directly into the modem or router, the next device in line is the firewall, which then connects to the switch where all of the computers are connected. By doing this, nothing comes in from the internet or goes out to the internet without first going through the firewall.

Off-Site Access

System users today are very mobile. Some study and prep off-site away from the church, some need access to congregant data from off-site, and more. There's more than one way to provide secure access from off-site. Here are a few of the most prevalent:

- *VPN Access.* This is probably the highest level of security for off-site access used by churches. A Virtual Private Network (VPN) is a private network even though it connects over the internet. A VPN accomplishes a higher level of security by creating an encrypted link, and requires the off-site system to run an app that has the digital key to unencrypt the link. Like all IT solutions, it has strengths and weaknesses:

    - *Strength*: VPNs provide the highest level of simple security for off-site access.

    - *Weakness*: VPNs require the off-site user to run an app to establish the VPN link, which is often more than what most in ministry can successfully cope with technologically. It's not that the app is difficult to run; it's that it requires an extra step to gain access that is often forgotten and generates frustration and support requests. VPNs are not intuitive.

- *Hosted databases.* Many ChMS databases are now hosted and available via browser (like Firefox, Safari, Edge, and so on). This automates the security when they are hosted on secure servers (an important requirement for a hosted ChMS). It has some strengths and weaknesses:

    - *Strength*: Data security access is automated, making it easily available to off-site staff and volunteers.

    – *Weakness*: The only data available is what is in the database. If there is additional data, like spreadsheets or documents, for example, they may not be available in this manner.

- *Remote Desktop Connection*. Data is available on a server that requires a connection, but the connection may not be highly secure. It looks like accessing data on a typical Windows server.

    – *Strength*: The interface is familiar and more intuitive than the process of establishing a VPN, and it looks like typical data access on a Windows server.

    – *Weakness*: Remote desktop sessions can be susceptible to what is called a "Man in the Middle Attack," in which someone monitoring internet traffic might intercept data being transferred. Some IT people combat this by adding a remote gateway that shields the actual server from the public, adding a security certificate, and securing the connection to help strengthen the security of this method.

- *Remote Data Synchronization*. Many use an app, like Dropbox or Owncloud, to synchronize data between devices. The net effect is that data can be stored on the mobile device *and* on the server, with changes made to it synchronized in real time if both are connected via network or internet connection.

    – *Strength*: This method, once it's configured, is fully automatic and requires no user intervention. On devices with storage capacity, like notebook computers, data can be stored locally on the mobile device and accessed as needed with or without an internet connection; changes will be synchronized automatically if or when connected.

– *Weakness*: Data on mobile devices increases risk if those devices are not adequately protected by their user, getting lost or stolen. Thus, security training is recommended. Also, some of these apps do not have good security, so if they require storing data on a public cloud server, they may not be a good solution. Dropbox is one whose security is questionable, which is why I prefer Owncloud (private cloud server with more tightly controlled access).

Mobile Device Vulnerability

By their very nature, mobile devices (smartphones, tablets, and notebook computers) are more vulnerable than other devices. They are more easily stolen or lost, so a strategy should be in place that allows a church to delete any sensitive data from a lost or stolen device the next time it connects to the internet. Some data synchronization services help, as do some mobile device operating systems. The strategy to delete sensitive data could be driven by the operating system and/or apps on the mobile device.

Churches should also have a defined process to delete sensitive data from an employee's mobile device upon resignation or termination.

Mobile devices also can be vulnerable when they connect to public WiFi hotspots. It is shockingly easy for a hacker to monitor the WiFi traffic happening in such an environment. The problem is that those who set up WiFi in public places rarely do so in a way that keeps hackers from seeing the data traffic from other devices.

The best policy is to not use public WiFi, but to instead connect to the internet through the WiFi hotspot capability in most smartphones. While doing so means it will use the data connection plan of the smartphone carrier, it is a small price (if there's even any cost at all!) to pay for the enhanced security and the protection it provides.

Internet of Things (IoT)

Many now have internet-connected devices in their homes. I'm not talking about computers, tablets, or smartphones—I'm referring to digital assistants (like Amazon Echo, Google Home, and Apple Home-Pod) and home devices and appliances like thermostats, refrigerators, trash cans, door locks, and more.

Upon purchase, most of these devices possess very limited security, and they're easy targets for internet programs (called bots) that want to access and control them.

In October of 2016 the largest Distributed Denial of Service (DDoS) attack (still true at the time of this book's publication) caused trouble for countless people worldwide. A DDoS attack occurs when web-connected servers, computers, or devices are hit with a huge number of false connection requests that essentially freeze out all legitimate requests.

In a forensic analysis after the DDoS attack, it was discovered that the attack was caused by a botnet (malware-controlled devices) made up of 100,000 devices! Further, analysts found that it could have been much worse because there were more than 500,000 devices in the botnet, and only 100,000 were used.

What should you do with your church's IoT devices? Here are some steps you can take to protect them from being accessed and controlled:

1. Contact your Internet Service Provider (ISP) and have them demonstrate to you that the modem or router they provide to connect you to the internet has security turned on and that it's set to the highest level (if there are multiple levels available).

2. Change the default password of the device.

3. Consider putting a firewall between your modem or router and the rest of your devices that connect to the internet.

CyberSecurity Risk Assessment

Churches also should consider hiring a firm that specializes in cybersecurity risk assessments to look at your systems and issue a report of strengths (what you're doing well) and weaknesses (opportunities for improvement). There's almost always *something* that can be improved, and having an expert set of eyes looking for those opportunities is helpful. You may want to check with your church or ministry's insurance carrier to see if it can recommend a cybersecurity firm to perform such an assessment. Doing so may even help reduce your insurance premiums!

CHAPTER 20

The Value of Standardization

|||||||||||||

Manage for results.

John Pearson [49]

|||||||||||||

When I was earning my business administration degree (with a focus on management), I formed a philosophy that shaped the way I approach the use of computers: *Good managers get the best possible results from limited resources.*

Good Management

As a Christian, I want to hear at the end of my earthly journey, "Well done, good and faithful servant. ... Come and share your master's happiness!"[50] My guess is that you feel the same way! So, how does a faithful servant, or in today's vernacular, a *good manager*, earn such praise?

The first important lesson is one taught by Jesus himself. He was a servant leader. The Last Supper is a great example—Jesus lowered himself to wash the feet of his friends. He even served the one he knew would betray him! Serving everyone with love and humility is essential.

---

[49] John Pearson, *Mastering the Management Buckets* (2008).
[50] Matthew 25:21

In every job, managers wrestle with limited resources. Whether it is restricted cash flow, teams that are too small for the task, equipment that is less than optimal, or something else, there is always at least one challenge. Yet, there is a job to do and goals to accomplish. Good managers, like race car drivers, do their best to keep RPMs and speeds as high as possible without blowing up the engine.

Similarly, a servant leader does his or her best to keep the team motivated and moving forward. Because servant leaders have an underlying posture of love and humility, they don't push their teams beyond what can be endured. They ensure team members are paid enough to care for themselves and their families, have enough downtime to get refreshed, and have appropriate tools available to help them with as few distractions as possible. That last point is where standardization has its impact.

Standardization

As my team and I began deploying larger and larger networks, we developed standards that helped us configure workstations. These standards helped us create workstations that fulfilled our clients' needs to accomplish their ministry goals without distractions. Over time, we found that some computer configuration settings helped and some hindered.

As we began to identify optimal configurations, we found it challenging to deliver those consistently on every workstation. It was easy to miss a setting or two on any given computer, and our lack of consistency caused *support tickets*. We saw the value in achieving standardization and needed a way to deliver it.[51]

51   Figure 8 is intentionally too small to easily read. The intent was to show how detailed our checklists are.

We developed a checklist system for each computer configuration: servers, Windows, Macs, and for each Operating System. Having a method of delivering a standardized configuration, we noticed that:

- Client satisfaction continued to increase, keeping pace as we began working for larger churches and ministries.
- *Support tickets* remained low despite the larger number of systems we were supporting.

Focusing on high-quality standardization helps keep our clients' support costs low. As we think of their call to build the Kingdom, that translates into fewer distractions and higher results. It means we're helping them achieve the best possible results with limited resources!

Figure 8: MBS' Setup Checklist for Windows 10

MBS' Setup Checklist

Here are some excerpts from our checklists for Windows 10 and macOS that you may find to be a helpful start:

- Windows 10
  - Windows Explorer Configuration & Actions
    - ❏ At the Root of the C drive, go to the View tab
    - ❏ Set View to List (this is a better view for most users)
    - ❏ Check File Name Extensions (most users want to see file extensions, and it helps with support)

- Control Panel Settings & Configuration
  - ❏ Sound: click the Sounds tab, then click Sound Scheme, then click No Sounds (helps to minimize office distractions)
  - ❏ Sound: while on the Sounds tab, uncheck Play Windows Startup Sound (helps to minimize office distractions)
  - ❏ Display: Adjust Resolution and/or Text Size
  - ❏ Screen Saver: set to none (helps reduce support issues)

- macOS
  - Finder Preferences
    - ❏ On the General tab, set New Finder windows to open to the user's home folder (speeds up finding files)
    - ❏ On the Sidebar Favorites tab, remove all checks except desktop and home folder (speeds up finding files and is less confusing)
    - ❏ With the Finder window open, click the View menu option (at top of the screen). Check Show as Columns, Show Path Bar, and Show Status Bar (columns is a better view for most users, and the Path Bar and Status Bar are very helpful in folder navigation and support)

  - Safari Preferences
    - ❏ Set downloads to automatically go to the Desktop (helps the user remember to delete downloads that are no longer needed, saving storage space)
    - ❏ Set the church's standard home page

We also include a section detailing which apps should be installed on every system (like Firefox, Microsoft Office, Thirtyseven4 for anti-malware, and so on).

This type of standardization helps users be more efficient, and it helps the support team when it responds to users requests. The users can change whatever they want, of course, but at least they each have a common starting point and are more predictable as a result.

The mistake most people make is not standardizing, which means every machine is different based on how it was set up by the manufacturer and may not be properly set up to run well for the user. Non-standardized systems tend to be more confusing to users and more challenging to support.

Mobile Device Management

Mobile Device Management, also known as MDM, is software designed to accomplish standardization across multiple operating systems and on various types of hardware. It is a great concept! Imagine managing any device in your system—whether face-to-face or remotely—and delivering operating system and app updates fully configured!

Many churches and corporations successfully use this technology. But our experience was different. We've tested various MDM solutions and have yet to find one that works efficiently for even *large* churches. We have set up MDMs to accomplish exactly what they promise to deliver, only to find that the time investment is too large—and the MDM gets stale unless one constantly keeps all aspects of it up to date.

We concluded MDM was more time-intensive than it was worth for even our largest clients (our largest has about 700 tablets, notebooks, and desktop computers). Doing it well seems to require devoting one team member to focus on making it work.

CHAPTER 21

Changing Paradigms: The Cloud, BYOD, Social Media, and AI

iIIIiiIIIiiIIIii

*The price of doing the same old thing is far
higher than the price of change.*

Bill Clinton [52]

iIIIiiIIIiiIIIii

Apple's iPhone and Google's Android have now been around for more than a decade. While there were smartphone-*like* devices (the Palm Treo, for example) prior to that, it wasn't until the iPhone that smartphones became mainstream. Those devices definitely changed the way we think about using technology today.

Churches occasionally ask me to help map out a ten-year IT strategy. In response, I point to recent technological changes, including smartphones and tablets, as examples of how fast things change. These churches then understand that ten years is too far out to plan! I suggest a two-year plan (the plan is a list of things they need to accomplish), which is based on a three- to five-year horizon (identifying the general direction where they want their ministry to go, sort of like a compass heading.

---

[52] President William Clinton, Public Papers of the Presidents of the United States, William J. Clinton, 1993 Book I: January 20 to July 31, 1993 (1994).

Four major paradigm changes are wildly affecting the planning for IT strategies and structures: the cloud, the "Bring Your Own Device" (BYOD) movement, social media, and artificial intelligence (AI).

The Cloud

The cloud is a paradigm shift that is already mature, and many churches are beginning to take advantage of its benefits.

Most of us, when we think of the cloud, think of social media platforms, email solutions, and online databases or backups. Those are important and make a difference. But the greater potential impact of the cloud is more than those services, and that impact is what really helps churches the most.

For decades, my firm has installed and configured local area networks (LANs) for churches and ministries nationwide. Those LANs require major capital investments in hardware, software, and engineering, which significantly impacts cash flow. The cloud can remove that large capital expense. This is the cloud's greatest potential for churches because it allows them to focus more of their cash flow toward ministry programming.

How much capital expense does it remove? Compare the costs in Figure 9 of two real situations for a large, single-site church (with about 2,000 in average weekly attendance). The ChMS provider already hosts the church's ChMS.

The immediate project savings is more than $40,000! You'll see in Figure 10 that if you include the cost of maintenance and support for both options, the monthly hosting fee never catches up to that savings! In fact, the spread is widening.

Item	Locally-Based	Cloud-Based
Hardware	**$12,830** 2 Servers (1 as a host & 1 for a bare metal backup), 2 UPSes, Backup Drive and Tapes	**None**
Software	**$3,415** Vmware vSphere Essentials, Windows 2012r2 with CALs, Exchange 2013 with 50 mailboxes , Veeam backup software	**$315** Exchange license & CALs
Engineering	**$30,970**	**$6,720**
Total Start	**$47,215**	**$7,035**
Monthly Hosting Fee	None	**$850**

Figure 9 – Local vs Cloud Hosted Cost Comparison

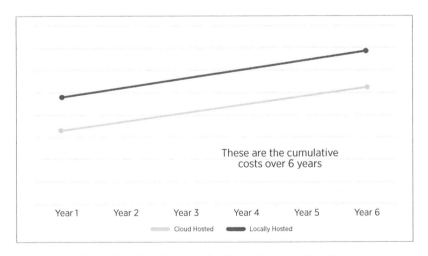

Figure 10 – Cloud vs. Locally Hosted Comparative Costs

The cloud provides churches with a major savings. It allows funds that would have been spent on hardware, software, and engineering to instead be invested elsewhere in ministry.

The key with cloud-hosted services is to keep your church's data private, safe, and secure. That requires some due diligence when selecting cloud-hosting vendor(s).

Chapter 15 explained how to select an outsource vendor (see "Who Can You Trust?" beginning on page 119), and in addition to that, add the following two criteria:

- *Private vs. Public Cloud.* There are two halves to the cloud: "public cloud" and "private cloud." Public cloud vendors allow anyone to create an account and to begin using their services. This includes Facebook, Twitter, Dropbox, and so on. Private cloud vendors require users to have been pre-approved and invited to access to connect to servers and services; they are not open and available to anyone. Understanding this difference is important because churches have a lot of sensitive data. With increasing threats toward sensitive data, safeguards are essential. Placing sensitive data only in a private cloud vendor's servers is an appropriate safeguard.

- *Datacenter Rating.* Datacenters are rated on their infrastructure redundancies: the more redundancies of power, internet trunks, and ability to manage environment (temperature and humidity), the greater the likelihood of uptime (staying up and running). Figure 11 is a quick explanation of the ratings a church should review before selecting one.[53] Higher-numbered ratings are preferable.

- I recommend a minimum datacenter certification of Tier 3, and I prefer Tier 4. Those tiers ensure the highest level of data availability.

- In addition, make certain your datacenter and/or host will keep your data in your country. Egypt, at the beginning of the Arab Spring[54] in late 2010, cut its internet connections to the world. If your church's data had been in Egypt at that time, you would have lost access to it until those connections were restored.

Tier Rating	Redundancy	% Uptime	Max Downtime
4	at least double redundancy, a.k.a. 2N+1 fault tolerance	**99.995%**	26.3 minutes annually
3	full redundancy, a.k.a. N+1 fault tolerance	**99.982%**	1.6 hours annually
2	partial redundancy	**99.749%**	22 hours annually
1	no redundancy (only one source of power, only one internet trunk, only one way to manage HVAC)	**99.671%**	22.8 hours annually

Figure 11 – Datacenter Tier Certifications

---

[53] Colocation America, *Uptime Institute's Tier Standard System,* http://colocationamerica.com/data-center/tier-standards-overview.htm.
[54] See en.wikipedia.org/wiki/Arab_Spring.

BYOD

BYOD is another paradigm shift gaining momentum. A BYOD situation is one in which a church team member uses his or her device instead of one supplied by the church. A small number of churches have begun taking advantage of its benefits so far, and that number is growing.

I am not sure why folks would prefer to use their own devices unless they would rather work in a different operating system (Windows vs. Mac or vice versa) than the one on the device supplied by the church. However, my firm even gets requests from individuals whose devices run the same OS as that of the church-supplied device!

This trend will likely continue and grow. The cloud's ubiquitous access to data and apps makes it a viable option.

BYOD makes most IT professionals uncomfortable. Historically, we have been able to keep devices not owned and configured by us off our networks. As IT people, we are responsible for protecting the data, so this has been the right thing to do. The policy has allowed us to protect data from malware and other threats. BYOD, though, increases threats to the data if the BYOD strategy is not implemented carefully.

I wrote an article in late 2013 because of this trend.[55] While researching that article I was surprised to learn the only corporate America BYOD policies in place at that time dealt with smartphones! My conclusion was that churches were leading this trend, perhaps because it's more acceptable to ask in a church setting, whereas maybe it's not okay to ask in a normal job setting (at least, not yet). Anyway, BYOD arrangements can work for churches—and save those churches

---

55   Nick Nicholaou, *Reasonable & Essential BYOD Policies,* MBS, Inc. (Sept. 4, 2013), http://mbsinc.com/reasonable-essential-byod-policies.

money. I recommend a minimum set of policies to protect the church and team members with BYOD arrangements.

In a recent Church IT Network online discussion, Jonathan Puddle (Director of Retail, Publishing, and Technology for the Catch the Fire ministry and a volunteer at his church) said his church is almost entirely BYOD! "We don't buy people machines anymore. We give them a cash rebate instead. … We mitigated against the cost of upgrades by pushing the whole thing to the users. Our staff buy their own personal machines and we provide a rebate. It has saved us tons. We did have to relax our management on the machines to accomplish this, but the end result has been great." The move saved the church a lot of money and increased its team members' satisfaction! What a great way to help achieve what Clif Guy said (see page 27) about trying to have a default "yes" posture!

BYOD is a growing technology trend, and churches are leading the way! Some implementation methods I am seeing churches use are:

- *SYOM, Spend Your Own Money.* This is the example mentioned above by Puddle. His church gives a rebate based on a formula that considers the team member's role on the church staff and a percentage of the purchase cost with a cap.

- *CYOM, Choose Your Own Machine.* Based on team members' roles on the church staff, they get a budget that can be applied to a list of pre-approved computer choices. If the system they select is beyond the established budget for that role, their department can choose to cover the additional cost out of its budget.

To make these types of arrangements work, the data needs better protection than it otherwise would need because of the increased threats that BYOD introduces. That protection should include better firewalls (don't just rely on the internet service provider's router settings) and malware protection (like Thirtyseven4[56]), as well as a better disaster recovery plan (a good backup strategy)—including more depth of backup history (I recommend a minimum of one month's backups for all churches, but more when BYOD is in play).

BYOD Policies

Since BYOD requests are on the rise, it's wise for churches to research this subject now and form policies *before* a team member asks to use his or her own device. Here is a starter list of what should be covered in a policy:

Team Member Responsibilities

- *To be productive.* Team members who request to use their personal computers and/or devices must understand that they are responsible to be productive. Thus any such BYOD request, if granted, will require that they be at least as productive as they would have been using the systems normally provided by the church. Setting the standards of productivity is the responsibility of management, and team members who are not as productive on their personally-owned computers and/or devices will be required to use church-provided systems.

- *To be cooperative.* Personally-owned computers and/or devices, if allowed to be used at work, must meet minimum standards. Those standards will be set and modified from time to time by the IT Department and may address minimum processor chipsets and operating system versions, amount of RAM and storage,

---

[56]   ThirtySeven4, LLC, www.thirtyseven4.com.

and the use of specific church-provided applications such as productivity suites (like Microsoft Office), anti-malware tools (like Thirtyseven4), email clients, and more. Use of substitute applications must be approved by both the IT Department and the team member's direct supervisor.

- *To be responsible.* The team member agrees to maintain their personally-owned computers and/or devices that have been approved for use at work at a level that meets or exceeds (1) productivity levels set by management and (2) the IT Department's minimum system requirements. The team member is responsible for any costs due to failed hardware, configuration and/or software issues, and theft or breakage.

- *To protect.* The team member agrees to maintain the security of their personally-owned computers and/or devices to protect the data and integrity of the church's systems; to let their supervisor and the IT Department know if their device has been lost or stolen within 24 hours; and to let the church install software that could delete the church's data if the church so desires, with or without notice. The team member agrees to submit their personally-owned computers and/or devices approved for use at work for inspection by the IT Department to confirm that the system is being properly protected against malware and other threats. The team member acknowledges that the church might see data and files that could otherwise be considered private, but agrees to hold the church harmless against any claims against loss of privacy in exchange for the church agreeing to allow the team member to use his or her personally-owned computers and/or devices for work.

Church Responsibilities

- *To provide a productive environment.* The church agrees to provide a suitable work area to help the team member be productive at levels required by management. In case the team member's personally-owned computers and/or devices are not available due to required repairs (for which the team member is responsible), the church will provide a substitute computer or device using church-owned computers and/or devices for a reasonable period of time.

- *To be reasonably accommodating.* When a team member requests permission to use their personally owned computer or device at work, the church agrees to be reasonably accommodating if the team member can demonstrate that their productivity will meet or exceed the productivity standards set by the church.

- *To be supportive.* The church is not responsible to support the team member's computer or device. However, the church will give help desk support at the same level as it does for church-owned computers on the use of software provided by the church.

- *To explain Exempt vs Non-Exempt issues.* Some team members are subject to overtime rules based on state and/or federal law. The church is responsible to explain the team member's exempt or non-exempt status, and how that impacts work time record-keeping.

Termination Procedures

If a team member is terminated by the church or initiates termination of the employment relationship, the team member agrees to remove all church-owned software and data from their personally-owned computer or device, or to provide it to the IT Department to allow the IT Department to remove the church-owned software and data.

Signed Acknowledgement

The team member and his or her supervisor will sign an agreement acknowledging the BYOD policies in place. The acknowledgement will also state that the church may modify the BYOD policy at any time and without prior notice.

Social Media

Many books and articles cover the pros and cons of social media (services like Facebook, Twitter, Instagram, and many more) for churches. For this book I simply want to focus on the point that having a website alone is no longer enough if you want to attract younger generations. Young adults and young families now look for Facebook pages and YouTube channels when they're searching for a new church or researching one.

Your church must adapt to this paradigm shift. Websites were important in the 1990s. A social media presence is important now. That doesn't mean eliminating your church's website. Rather, it is important your church communicate via all of the "channels" your community uses: websites *and* social media sites.

Artificial Intelligence

A study conducted several years ago at the University of Southern California using Artificial Intelligence (AI) revealed surprising results in the treatment of military veterans with Post Traumatic Stress Disorder (PTSD)[57].

Researchers found that veterans with PTSD were more willing to share their issues with a *virtual human* than they were with real humans![58]

Could this technology be used in ministry? One very large US Christian ministry is beginning to test AI in a manner similar to the way USC found it productive. This is brand new on our ministry radar, and we'll continue to keep our eyes on it!

---

57 Anna-Catherine Brigida, *A Virtual Therapist,* USC Viterbi School of Engineering (Oct. 18, 2013), https://viterbi.usc.edu/news/news/2013/a-virtual-therapist.htm.

58 Joseph Frankel, *PTSD Treatment: How AI Is Helping Veterans With Post-Traumatic Stress Disorder,* Newsweek (Oct. 12, 2017), https://www.newsweek.com/ptsd-treatment-how-ai-could-help-veterans-post-traumatic-stress-disorder-682857.

CHAPTER 22

Strategies for Solo Pastors

‖‖‖‖‖‖‖‖‖‖‖

Because God gave you your makeup and
superintended every moment of your
past, including all the hardship, pain, and
struggles, He wants to use your words in
a unique manner. No one else can speak
through your vocal chords, and, equally
important, no one else has your story.

Charles R. Swindoll [59]

‖‖‖‖‖‖‖‖‖‖‖

Many pastors serve in churches where they are the only paid staff member—or maybe one of two paid staff members. As such, they don't have the resources available to them that those who serve in larger churches possess, and their use of technology is often more of a challenge because they can't use enterprise-class strategies. In fact, their work computers are more akin to consumer-class home solutions, and they tend to be at the mercy of whoever's available to give them support when needed.

---

[59]   Charles R. Swindoll, *Stones of Remembrance: Bible Study Guide* (1988).

Some of that is changing, and I hope to address here some of the ways solo pastors can employ strategies to improve the reliability of their technology.

Buying Hardware

Price is a big factor, but support is an even bigger one. Look for a vendor who can support you without forcing you to ship in your computer for repairs. Best Buy has its Geek Squad, and Office Depot offers its Workonomy Tech Services. Look for a support service like one of these—something that will be available as conveniently as possible.

Some things to insist on when you make your purchase:

- An educational discount if you're a student or professor.

- A pro version of the operating system (you definitely do not want the "Home" or "Student" versions).

- Assistance with removing all "trialware" that comes with your computer. (The merchant often does this for a small fee, but it's worth it. Maybe you can negotiate and get it thrown in with the purchase!)

- The inclusion of extended warranty care that includes coverage for accidents involving mobile devices if, for instance, the device is a notebook or tablet.

Buying Software

Software makes it possible to get your work done. If the purchase is made by your church, you may qualify for charity pricing. If you're a student or professor, your purchase may qualify for an educational discount. Again, though, only purchase enterprise or pro versions of the software if possible. In addition, some of today's operating systems already include apps that may be adequate for word processing, spreadsheets, and so on.

Resources that Can Help

If your church is affiliated with a denomination or movement, contact them and ask if they have technology resources and solutions available to help you. Many do, and even if they come for a fee, they are worth buying.

While at a denominational conference not long ago, we talked with a lot of solo pastors. The issues they dealt with were so sad, and their issues impeded their effectiveness. We felt like the Lord was challenging us to use our resources to help.

In response, we put together a solution called Missional IT[60]. It makes it possible for a solo pastor to use a ministry-appropriate email address (like first.last@ourchurch.net) that is also effectively filtered for SPAM. It also includes a service that works simply for securely backing up church files like sermons, board meeting minutes, and so on.

Lastly, one final resource worth mentioning is the collection of hundreds of articles I have written over the years. Many are available on my firm's website for free! When you have an IT-related question, you may find the answer at www.mbsinc.com/articles-search!

Solo pastors are not alone! In Chapter 15, I mention four firms that focus on serving Christian churches and ministries. Contact them and ask if they have ways they can help a solo pastor.

---

60   MBS, Inc., http://www.mbsinc.com/services/missional-it.

Glossary of Terms

A

AI, Artificial Intelligence. A type of programming that allows an app to respond in context to input as though interpreting and reasoning.

Apps. The applications used on computers to accomplish tasks. Also referred to as software.

Auto Attendant. An internal telephone system's receptionist or operator that is *not* a live person, but instead is a recorded voice offering a set of menu options to the caller.

B

Backup. The practice of making copies of data as part of a disaster recovery plan.

BCP, Business Continuity Plan. A detailed plan of how an organization will continue operations during a disaster.

Bot. A usually malicious program running on the internet looking for computer and system vulnerabilities.

Botnet. A network of malware-controlled devices.

BYOD, Bring Your Own Device. Allowing organization team members to use their own computers rather than requiring them to only use those provided by the organization.

C

ChMS, Church Management Software. Database systems that help churches track congregants' contact information, contributions, attendance, and volunteer involvement. Some ChMS solutions also provide an accounting solution unique to the accounting needs of churches.

CYOM, *Choose Your Own Machine.* Allowing organization team members to choose their computers from a menu of options rather than requiring them to use a specific configuration.

Church IT Network. The Church IT Network, a.k.a. CITRT, is a group of church-specific IT people who gather to help each other with proven solutions and encourage each other through the challenges of managing IT in churches.

The Cloud. There are many ways to define the Cloud. The easiest definition is that the data and apps are stored and accessed online; these are often referred to as hosted data and apps.

CFO, *Chief Financial Officer.* The primary officer of a corporation responsible for managing the corporation's finances.

CIO, *Chief Information Officer.* The primary officer of a corporation responsible for managing all of the corporation's technology. This position is also often referred to as the CTO, or Chief Technology Officer.

COO, *Chief Operations Officer.* The primary officer of a corporation responsible for managing the corporation's day-to-day operations.

CTO, *Chief Technology Officer.* The primary officer of a corporation responsible for managing all of the corporation's technology. This position is also often referred to as the CIO, or Chief Information Officer.

D

Datacenter. Any place that has servers can be referred to as a data-center. However, the term usually refers to a location that is very large and houses thousands of servers.

DDoS Attack, *Distributed Denial of Service.* An internet attack against computers, servers, and internet-connected devices designed to overwhelm its target with requests for attention so that its normal uses are jammed.

DRP, Disaster Recovery Plan. A detailed plan of how an organization will recover from a disaster.

DNS, Domain Name System. The worldwide system that facilitates internet connectivity by storing data about how to connect to every website, email server, and so on.

E

Encryption. A technological scrambling of data that requires a digital key to unscramble and access encrypted data. The key is provided by running an app, whether it's part of the operating system or independent of the operating system.

ESXi. VMware's hypervisor.

Ethernet. A type of cable to connect computers and other devices to the network or to the internet. Ethernet cables have modular-type plugs that "clip" in to their socket.

F

Firewall. A hardware or software solution to keep intruders out of a computer system.

G

GDPR, General Data Protection Regulation. The European Union's 2018 law requiring companies to allow someone to disappear from their databases.

GUI, Graphical User Interface. The presentation by an app of its features and data on a computer monitor or display; how a computer user interfaces with the computer app.

H

Hardware. Physical computers and other IT infrastructure devices.

Host. A server-class physical computer that has a hypervisor installed, allowing it to *host* multiple virtual (non-physical) servers.

Hosted. The location of the servers, data, and apps; hosted usually refers to an off-site location, though when located in-house it can be referred to as *locally hosted*.

HyperV. Microsoft's hypervisor.

Hypervisor. An app that allows a physical computer to be configured as a host for multiple virtual computers.

I

IGMP (Internet Group Management Protocol). A communications protocol that facilitates aggressively managed multicast data. Switches use IGMP to "listen" to the "conversation" between devices to actively manage/lighten the network load.

Infrastructure. Like roads and utilities are part of a geographic region's infrastructure, the servers, switches, and cabling that facilitate the access and sharing of data are called IT infrastructure.

Insource. Hiring employees to do tasks because the tasks are an organization's mission or core skill set.

IP, Internet Protocol. The method used to transmit data from one computer to another using those machines' IP Addresses (unique sets of numbers that identify the computer on a network or on the internet). The term IP is often coupled with another term, TCP (Transmission Control Protocol) in the format of TCP/IP.

ISO. A file that is an image of a CD or DVD that can be mounted logically just as though it was physical media. You can also burn an ISO file to optical media and run it that way.

ISP, Internet Service Provider. The company providing your internet service.

IT, Information Technology. The profession and application of computers to store, recall, transmit, and manipulate data in an organization.

J

Jumbo Frame (aka 'jumbos'). A setting allowing a packet of data to contain more than 1,500 bytes, increasing the limit as high as 9,000 bytes. Basically, this allows a *frame* of information to carry more information, referred to as the *payload*, in a single frame, improving performance of fast networks.

L

LAN, Local Area Network. A connected group of computers and devices at an organization, usually located at the organization's site.

Licensing. The terms of the legal permission that gives the purchaser of apps and hardware the right to use their purchase within certain limits and sometimes with certain restrictions.

Live Attendant. An internal telephone system's receptionist or operator that is a live person.

Local Admin. A desktop or notebook computer setting that gives the person using it the ability to make modifications, like adding an app. This capability sometimes is reserved only for the professional IT staff. Local Admin rights do not impact a user's network rights or permissions.

M

Malware. Apps that are written for the express purpose of destroying data and systems, or holding them captive for ransom.

MBS, Ministry Business Services, Inc. The IT consulting firm founded by the author, Nick Nicholaou. (*www.mbsinc.com*)

MDM, Mobile Device Management. Software designed to manage computer and device configurations and patches. See section beginning on page 159 for a more complete explanation.

MFA, Multi-Factor Authentication. The requirement of using as many as three identification verification factors when logging in to a system. This is related to 2FA (Two-Factor Authentication). See section beginning on page 146 for a more complete explanation.

Mission Critical. Something that, if it fails, will result in the failure of the organization's operations.

N

NAS, Network Attached Storage. A server-type device on a network that provides storage, acting like an external hard drive. NAS servers predate SANs, and provide file-level access to their contents.

NOS, Network Operating System. Similar to the operating system on a computer, this operating system is what makes it possible for the computer to function as a server on a network server *vs* a regular computer.

O

Outsource. Hiring non-employees to do tasks that are not an organization's mission or core skill set.

OS, Operating System. Every computer and device runs a foundational software that enables it to run apps and meet the needs of its user. Examples are Windows, Mac OSX, Android, and iOS.

P

PBX, Private Branch Exchange. Internal telephone systems typified by a central operator or receptionist.

PCI Compliance. The credit card industry's requirement for any organization processing credit card and debit card transactions.

Private Cloud. Cloud-based servers and services only accessible to those who were pre-approved to access and use them.

Productivity Software. A set of apps that usually includes word processing, spreadsheets, and other modules.

Public Cloud. Cloud-based servers and services accessible to any who would like to connect to them, such as Facebook, Dropbox, Instagram, and so on.

S

SAN, Storage Area Network. Similar to a NAS, a SAN is a server-like device that is like a large external hard drive that network users can access. It has more redundancy and safety built into it than a NAS, and is faster. SANs' contents are at the block level vs. the file level, thus requiring a server or some kind of client to access the files stored on them.

Silos of Data. When team members use various databases—even spreadsheets or documents—to manage their ministries, each is a silo of data. If those silos don't have the ability to exchange and coordinate data, the church sacrifices an important synergy in accomplishing its mission.

Softphone. An app that replaces the physical telephone handset.

Software. The applications used on computers to accomplish tasks, also referred to as apps.

SSID, Service Set Identifier. The name of the WiFi signals available to connect a device to.

SYOM, Spend Your Own Money. One of the BYOD strategies in which church team members contribute to the cost of their computers or mobile devices.

T

Trialware. Software that comes on new, consumer-class computers. The software providers underwrite some of the computer cost if the manufacturer includes their solution with the computer, but the programs are just trial versions that eventually expire and must be purchased if continued use is desired. Two big problems with trialware: one, they're rarely ever worth using, and two, they don't always *cleanly* uninstall, causing future problems.

V

Virtual Host. A server-class physical computer that has a hypervisor installed, allowing it to *host* multiple virtual (non-physical) servers.

Virtualization. Computers that are not actual physical computers but are virtual configurations that act like separate computers made possible by an app referred to as a hypervisor.

VoIP, Voice Over Internet Protocol. Telephone systems that transmit calls using internet technology rather than traditional telephone technology.

VPN, Virtual Private Network. A secure method of accessing data, usually from off-site, that involves encrypting the communication signal.

Vsphere. VMware's hypervisor.

W

WAP, Wireless Access Point. The WiFi radios that broadcast WiFi signals

X

XenServer. Citrix's hypervisor.

#s

2FA, Two-Factor Authentication. The requirement of using as many as two identification verification factors when logging in to a system. This is related to MFA (Multi-Factor Authentication). See section beginning on page 146 for a more complete explanation.

Table of References

This is a list of people and ministries who were quoted or referenced through this book.

T
The Church IT Network – *66, 111*
The Church Network – *66, 111*
ThirtySeven4.com – *50*
Twain, Mark – *77*

V
Veeam – *128, 130, 133, 163*

W
Wall Street Journal – *8*
Warner, Greg – *128*
Wikipedia – *18*
Willow Creek Association – *7*

About the Author

Nick Bruce Nicholaou grew up in an agnostic home and is the oldest of three and the only son of a couple that began their marriage very young. He chose a childhood path that destined him to an early grave, and he would have ended up there if the Lord had not gotten his attention at the age of twenty-one.

When God got a hold of his life, he gave Nick a thirst and hunger for the Scriptures and tied him to a group of believers who helped shape his desire to serve God in every way possible—however the Lord wanted.

After college, Nick was hired into executive service in the automobile manufacturing industry where he was tasked to help dealerships improve their customer satisfaction and success. Because he had to influence independent business owners to change some of what they did and how they did it, the Lord used that time to develop Nick's consulting skills.

When Nick was in college—before the advent of the personal computer—he believed computers could be great tools to help accomplish many tasks better and more efficiently. While majoring in business administration with a management focus, he took a computer course every semester so he could gain access to the school's mainframe computer system.

Just months into his marriage, while in devotions one day, Nick sensed the Lord telling him he wanted Nick to do something different. *This must be the result of last night's pepperoni*, Nick thought. But then it happened the next two days also! So, Nick decided he needed to tell his wife, Grace, even though she might think him weird. She responded, "I've been getting the *same thing!*" So they determined to discover what that meant by researching the needs of churches and how the Lord might use them to help meet those needs.

Their sense was that he wanted to take Nick's business management skills and Grace's accounting skills (she's a CPA who has focused her practice on serving Christian churches and ministries) and use them to help Christian churches and ministries across the United States. That was in 1986. They have been fulfilling that call ever since!

Nick often says that it is amazing what God can do with someone who is willing and available to serve him, however he wants! And, that he, himself, is proof!

Made in the USA
Monee, IL
14 July 2022

99719985R10105